Praise for Sundays

"If there were an antidote for reclaiming peace in our families and the world, Donna-Marie just wrote the book on it. *Reclaiming Sundays* is truly the answer to build and rebuild the domestic church."
—LEAH DARROW,
author of *The Other Side of Beauty*

"What a delightful book! Filled with great ideas of how to make Sundays special, *Reclaiming Sundays* is a treasure trove of prayers, reflections, and family activities to help every family delight in the Day of the Lord. As a priest, I will be recommending this book to families and newly married couples. I am certain this book will be a blessing for families and society in general."
—FR. DONALD CALLOWAY, MIC,
author of *10 Wonders of the Rosary*

"Finally, there's a helpmate for making Sundays holy again! Donna-Marie has done a spectacular job of bringing to light the vital importance of the Lord's Day to our spiritual, mental, and physical health and offering a practical, useful, and fun resource for reclaiming Sundays for ourselves and those we love. Keep *Reclaiming Sundays* handy —you'll be referring back to it often!"
—MARGE STEINHAGE FENELON,
speaker and best-selling author of *Forgiving Mother, My Queen, My Mother: A Living Novena*, and *Our Lady, Undoer of Knots: A Living Novena*

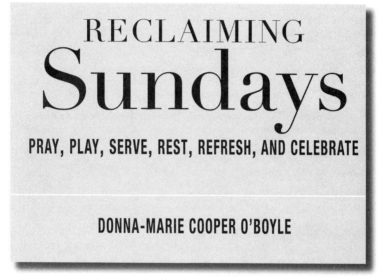

RECLAIMING
Sundays

PRAY, PLAY, SERVE, REST, REFRESH, AND CELEBRATE

DONNA-MARIE COOPER O'BOYLE

PARACLETE PRESS
BREWSTER, MASSACHUSETTS

2020 First Printing

Reclaiming Sundays: Pray, Play, Serve, Rest, Refresh, and Celebrate

Copyright © 2020 by Donna-Marie Cooper O'Boyle

ISBN 978-1-64060-147-5

All quotations from Holy Scripture are taken from the New Revised Standard Version Bible: Catholic Edition, copyright 1989, 1993, Division of Christian Education of the National Council of the Churches of Christ in the United States of America. Used by permission. All rights reserved.

Quotations marked (CCC) are taken from the English translation of the Catechism of the Catholic Church for use in the United States of America Copyright © 1994, United States Catholic Conference, Inc. – Libreria Editrice Vaticana. Used with Permission.

Quotations from Writings, Encyclicals, and Apostolic Exhortations by several Popes are © Libreria Editrice Vaticana and are used with Permission.

The Paraclete Press name and logo (dove on cross) are trademarks of Paraclete Press, Inc.

Library of Congress Cataloging-in-Publication Data

Names: O'Boyle, Donna-Marie Cooper, author.
Title: Reclaiming Sundays : pray, play, serve, rest, refresh, and celebrate
  / Donna-Marie Cooper O'Boyle.
Description: Brewster : Paraclete Press, 2020. | Summary: "By committing to
  reclaiming your family Sundays, you will be guided to fight the unending
  busyness and things which take us away from God. Through using this
  book, families will be helped to recognize the importance of growing
  together spiritually, physically, and emotionally on the Lord's Day
  within the blessedness of their family. You'll be guided by words of
  wisdom from the Catechism and Church teachings, which tell us how to
  slow down and rest on Sunday"-- Provided by publisher.
Identifiers: LCCN 2019031420 | ISBN 9781640601475 (trade paperback)
Subjects: LCSH: Sunday. | Families--Religious life. | Catholic
  Church--Doctrines.
Classification: LCC BV130 .O26 2020 | DDC 263/.3--dc23
LC record available at https://lccn.loc.gov/2019031420

10 9 8 7 6 5 4 3 2 1

Published by Paraclete Press
Brewster, Massachusetts
www.paracletepress.com

Printed in the United States of America

With great love to my children:
Justin, Chaldea, Jessica, Joseph, and Mary-Catherine
And to my grandchildren: Shepherd and Leo

CONTENTS

INTRODUCTION

Vivid memories of my Sundays growing up in a large family are etched upon my heart. My mother made sure that all her eight "ducklings" were home whenever possible. We went to Mass in the morning and came home to enjoy a pancake-and-egg breakfast. That was after one of us kids ran out to the chicken coop, dodging our protective rooster to collect the fresh eggs warm from the nests. Relatives stopped by later on, and we often played board games together. Later in the afternoon, my mother made a nice family dinner and expected that we would all be at the table to enjoy it together. It was not an option.

Those were the days! Times have changed. Sunday in many families has become just another day. It can be a significant challenge these days to honor and to live the Third Commandment to keep Sunday holy and as a day of rest. Years ago, in a simpler lifestyle, there weren't as many distractions bombarding parents. Today's families have a tendency to be stretched—constantly beckoned by technology—and are usually over-active. They might not give much thought to making Sunday the special day that it is meant to be.

As we rush around, trying to accomplish so much, our busyness typically spills into our Sundays. That's a problem because often it becomes impossible to carve out the necessary time to rest and recharge our batteries. There's no time left! But let's hang in here because God has given us a way to do so. This book will help you to happily reclaim your Sundays.

God has set aside a full day each week for us to worship, rest, be refreshed, serve, and grow in holiness. At times, we have totally missed God's invitation because we either forgot, we weren't listening, or we were just too busy. We also need the reminders to slow down since life is packed with events.

The Third Commandment is the reminder, "Remember the Sabbath day, to keep it holy." The Catholic Catechism tells us, "The institution of

Sunday helps all 'to be allowed sufficient rest and leisure to cultivate their familial, cultural, social, and religious lives'" (CCC, no. 2194). Clearly our Church wants us to slow down on Sundays. Most importantly, God wants us to. When families make the (sometimes heroic) effort to put on the brakes to experience the proper rest and refreshment they are meant to enjoy on Sundays, they will not only feel healthier and more balanced; they will be better equipped to fulfill their duties throughout the week.

God knew what he was doing when he created Sundays! Scripture tells us, "For in six days the LORD made heaven and earth, the sea, and all that is in them, but rested the seventh day; therefore the LORD blessed the sabbath day and consecrated it" (Exod. 20:11).

WHAT TO EXPECT FROM THIS BOOK

Family togetherness through meaningful activities will be emphasized throughout this Catholic family guide to help you to reclaim your Sundays. By committing to reclaiming your family Sundays, you will be guided to fight the scores of temptations from the secular culture, which urges everyone to become preoccupied with unending busyness and things that take us away from God and immerse us into a darkened culture. At the same time, through using this book, families will be helped in a great way to recognize the importance of growing together spiritually, physically, and emotionally on the Lord's Day within the blessedness of their family.

You'll be guided to words of wisdom from the Catechism and Church teachings, which tell us how to slow down and rest on Sunday. For example: "On Sundays and other holy days of obligation, the faithful are to refrain from engaging in work or activities that hinder the worship owed to God, the joy proper to the Lord's Day, the performance of the works of mercy, and the appropriate relaxation of mind and body" (CCC, no. 2185).

HOW TO USE THIS BOOK

Each Sunday's compilation will include an inspirational verse to set the tone for the day, original or traditional family prayers to be said together, and suggested meaningful and fun activities; these could be a work of mercy, a simple craft or project, or a story idea. There are mini teachings about the family and the domestic church woven throughout and, occasionally, a suggested simple recipe to make together.

HAVE FUN!

There are absolutely no rules in following this book. Keep *Reclaiming Sundays* nearby and handy to be reminded to slow down on Sundays and to **reclaim** them as the holy and restful days they are meant to be. Perhaps you will keep it in your kitchen or dining room to pick up and discuss at the table.

I invite you to turn to this book as often as needed for ideas for family togetherness, ministry, and fun while observing the holiness of Sunday. Skip around in the book to find whatever suits your family the particular Sunday that you wish to observe. For instance, you might be in the mood to celebrate a Sunday in a "Marian" sort of way. Simply skip to that section of the book and choose a Marian Sunday. You will discover many categories that are divided into seasons, ideas, and situations from which to choose.

You certainly don't have to do every single suggestion listed for each Sunday reflection. However, I encourage you to read the entire chapter each week so that you won't miss the "mini teaching" and other tips and encouragement for your domestic church. I recommend that you take a look at the book throughout the week and pick out a Sunday theme that you'd like to put into practice the following Sunday. You'll be prepared in every way and hopefully enjoy a stress-free week while you look forward to your family Sunday! For fun, and perhaps for a challenge, pick a chapter at random and strive to carry it out with your family; this might mean pushing a bit beyond your comfort zone.

I pray that you'll find this book flexible, practical, and most of all, a welcoming tool to inspire your family to observe Sundays in a manner that is pleasing to God and nurturing for your family as well. All the while, you are sure to carry down family traditions from the past and possibly create new ones together. Enjoy every bit of it!

My heart holds fond memories of my family Sundays when I was a child. In addition to the traditions we kept each Sunday that I mentioned earlier, we never failed to have our treat of a dish of ice cream every Sunday evening! Let us together RECLAIM our Sundays! May God bless your journey.

Spring Sundays

"May my teaching drop like the rain, my speech condense like the dew; like gentle rain on grass, like showers on new growth. For I will proclaim the name of the Lord; ascribe greatness to our God!"
—Deuteronomy 32:2–3

I love the season of spring and its warm breezes on my face as I take a stroll to observe beautiful new life. As the winter's fierce, cold winds subside and springtime starts to come forth from the shadows, we look forward in hope to the luscious blooms of crocuses, tulips, and daffodils we will see bursting from the earth after a such a frigid winter (depending upon where we live). The buds on the trees bring us the hope of the beauty we'll soon see as magnolias, dogwoods, and other beautiful trees and shrubs begin to unveil their beautiful blossoms.

We generally think of spring as a time of rebirth because we can see it in nature around us and because we can feel the warmer temperatures. What a beautiful example for us to see God's handiwork—once again reminding us that he is God and he makes all things new.

Ponder ways in which you can become more alive in your Faith this springtime. As you pray, allow God to work on your heart and make you new so you will be an exemplary Christian example to your family and others in this marvelous season of hope.

Planting Seeds of Faith
Sunday

"Now the parable is this: The seed is the word of God. The ones on the path are those who have heard; then the devil comes and takes away the word from their hearts, so that they may not believe and be saved. The ones on the rock are those who, when they hear the word, receive it with joy. But these have no root; they believe only for a while and in a time of testing fall away. As for what fell among the thorns, these are the ones who hear; but as they go on their way, they are choked by the cares and riches and pleasures of life, and their fruit does not mature. But as for that in the good soil, these are the ones who, when they hear; but as they go on their way, they are choked by the cares and riches and pleasures of life, and their fruit does not mature. But as for that in the good soil, these are the ones who, when they hear the word, hold it fast in an honest and good heart, and bear fruit with patient endurance."
—Luke 8:11–15

FAMILY MORNING PRAYER

Read the verse above and pray the Morning Offering together as a family.

Morning Offering: Dear Lord Jesus, thank you for the gift of today—your Sunday. Please guide our family as we strive to grow closer to you and to one another. Open our hearts and teach us to be more generous with our time. Open our eyes to discover opportunities to love others. Amen.

Pray: *Our Father, Hail Mary, Glory Be.*

REFLECT

Spring is the perfect time of year to plant seeds of Faith in your family's hearts! Everything around us in nature reaches toward heaven. New growth of flowers and plants reminds us of our wonderful Creator who provides a bountiful earth for us. What will we do with it? Will we enjoy it and care for it? You might also ask yourself another question: What seeds of Faith might you endeavor to plant in the hearts of those around you? Ponder and put your ideas and inspiration into action! Read Luke 8:11–15 to prepare your heart. Read it slowly and take a few minutes to ponder its meaning. Impress upon the family the need to nourish the "soil" of their hearts with prayer and sound teachings to allow the "seeds" that Jesus sows in our hearts to take root and flourish. You can also read the verse and discuss with the family at the breakfast, lunch, or dinner table.

CHOOSE AN ACTIVITY

Planting and illustrating: Since we are talking about planting seeds, as well as God's bountiful earth, you might plant seeds with your family today, or devise ways in which your family will help take care of God's creation. In addition, you could have the children make an illustration with crayons or paints after listening to the poem "A Prayer in Spring" (see below in the "Mini Teaching" section). Perhaps they can compose their own poem or verse. Do this as a family, or allow each child to write or create their own to share with everyone afterward.

Quiz activity: Check out how observant the kids are. Allow them to stretch their brains a little by asking them a few questions:

What have you noticed today that is different from yesterday?
What have you noticed in nature lately that makes you think?
    List three things.
What do you like best about this time of year?

NOTE TO PARENTS AND GRANDPARENTS

Talk to the children about doing their best to pay attention to life all around them. If they are too busy with media or television, they can get caught up with senseless or useless matters instead of the life that God provides for them. When distracted or preoccupied with many things, they might miss opportunities to have meaningful conversations with family members or others. As well, they can lose the chance to observe the awe and wonder of springtime blossoming around them.

MINI TEACHING

Read to the children the poem "A Prayer in Spring" by Robert Frost. While they might not be familiar with the style, it is a classic. Help them to understand the meaning. Robert Frost points out springtime's beauty. You can encourage the kids to be more attentive and appreciative of God's creation.

A Prayer in Spring

Oh, give us pleasure in the flowers to-day;
And give us not to think so far away
As the uncertain harvest; keep us here
All simply in the springing of the year.

Oh, give us pleasure in the orchard white,
Like nothing else by day, like ghosts by night;
And make us happy in the happy bees,
The swarm dilating round the perfect trees.

And make us happy in the darting bird
That suddenly above the bees is heard,
The meteor that thrusts in with needle bill,
And off a blossom in mid-air stands still.

For this is love and nothing else is love,
The which it is reserved for God above
To sanctify to what far ends He will,
But which it only needs that we fulfil.[1]

PONDER

Take time to ponder ways in which you can become more alive in your Faith this springtime. Sunday is a perfect day to ponder such things. As you pray, allow God to heal you of any inner wounds and make you new so that you will be an exemplary Christian example to your family and others in this marvelous season of hope. Have fun with the family. Smile! Make room for playing and laughing! All the while, you are creating marvelous experiences and memories.

FAMILY EVENING PRAYER

to be prayed each evening this week

Dear Lord, thank you for the blessings of this day—your day. If we have failed you in any way, please forgive us, Lord. If we have failed one another by not taking care of our responsibilities, please forgive us, Lord. Please help us to grow in holiness each day. We love you! Amen.

Pray: *Our Father, Hail Mary, Glory Be.*

CHAPTER 2

New Birth Sunday

"Create in me a clean heart, O God, and put a new and right spirit within me."
—Psalm 51:10

FAMILY MORNING PRAYER

Read the verse above and pray the Morning Offering together as a family.

Morning Offering: Dear Lord Jesus, thank you for the gift of today—your Sunday. Please guide our family as we strive to grow closer to you and to one another. Open our hearts and teach us to be more generous with our time. Open our eyes to discover opportunities to love others. Amen.

Pray: *Our Father, Hail Mary, Glory Be.*

REFLECT

The season of spring certainly reminds us of new birth whenever we take a look at nature blooming around us. As well, we can consider and pray for the new births of babies coming into the world this spring. We can also lament and pray to make reparation for the countless innocent lives that have been lost and will be lost through abortion. While the abortion subject might be too sensitive or confusing for little children, teenagers and adults can make a conscious effort to support and pray for human life from conception to natural death.

CHOOSE AN ACTIVITY

Baby shower: Consider a family project or activity that supports life. How about arranging a "baby shower" that can be held at your parish in the near future? I have organized this at my parish in the past and was delighted to see how many folks wanted to help. You can seek permission from your pastor, put a notice in the parish bulletin (at least a month in advance with reminders as you get closer to the date). Ask for donations of new baby items (specifying a few important ones), noting the dates and times for drop off. You and your family, as well as any others you might enlist to help can collect the gifts and bring them to a local pro-life pregnancy center. They will surely be delighted, as well as grateful to receive the practical gifts.

Build a nest: If you choose to "build a nest" together as mentioned in the "Mini Teaching" below, you will need a clear jar and some wooden toothpicks.

NOTE TO PARENTS AND GRANDPARENTS

Talk to the children about the importance of always treating every person with charity. We have not walked in their shoes. Explain to the kids that sometimes people act out in anger or grumpiness due to their life's hurts and that we should never retaliate. Instead, we can pray for them and even offer a kind word or a smile. Christ's love shown through us to others can help transform hearts. As well, encourage them to think about their spiritual lives each day and the need to work at their salvation. Find simple ways to impart this message. You could use examples or stories to illustrate this point.

MINI TEACHING

Read and in your own words explain the teaching to the children.

What can we learn from birds? Since we are in the season of spring, we can observe new life. We might observe a mother and father bird building a nest for their future baby birds. I have watched with fascination House Wrens building nests together. I find it delightful that the male wren finds several nesting places in early spring, carrying twigs in his beak, managing to fit them into the small holes of the birdhouse or crevice.

The male wren belts out a song to attract a female. The female wren comes around to investigate and chooses which nest will be their home. After the male has successfully attracted the female to his masterpiece, the remainder of the nest-building is done by the female, who wants her nest just right. After much effort, the nest is ready for her to lay eggs. After the eggs hatch, both parent birds feed the babies with insects and berries, and they each take care of them.

You might find an occasion to look around your surroundings to scout out bird's nests, being careful not to disturb them. One spring, I observed at least four House Wren families in various places around my house. You can research about birds and share your findings with the family. Explain to the children that they work hard at finding and fetching twigs and soft moss and feathers, to cushion the nest for the eggs. Many twigs are required. Building the nest is much like working at our spiritual lives. Encourage the children to try hard each day to "build" upon their spiritual life. They can think of each good deed and prayer as another "twig" in their spiritual "nest building."

Build a nest: Have the children draw an illustration of a bird's nest. Another idea is to place an empty clear jar or container on the kitchen counter with a number of wooden toothpicks (or other similar items) in a nearby container. Each time your child accomplishes a good deed, work of mercy, or has prayed an extra prayer, with your permission (and supervision), he or she may add a "twig" to the jar. Everyone can build the "nest" together. Perhaps when enough "twigs" are in the nest, you can treat the family to an ice cream cone, popcorn, or a fun board game!

PONDER

Ponder ways in which you can become more alive in your Faith this springtime—in this marvelous season of hope. When time allows, check out "Building Your Domestic Church" at the conclusion of this book for an idea you can put into place. Have fun with the family. Don't take yourself too seriously! Yes, life is serious, but we need to make room for playing and laughing!

FAMILY EVENING PRAYER

to be prayed each evening this week

Dear Lord, thank you for the blessings of this day—your day. If we have failed you in any way, please forgive us, Lord. If we have failed one another by not taking care of our responsibilities, please forgive us, Lord. Please help us to grow in holiness each day. We love you! Amen.

Pray: *Our Father, Hail Mary, Glory Be.*

⚫ CHAPTER 3 ⚫

Growing in Faith Sunday

"As you therefore have received Christ Jesus the Lord, continue to live your lives in him, rooted and built up in him and established in the faith, just as you were taught, abounding in thanksgiving."
—Colossians 2:6–7

FAMILY MORNING PRAYER

Read the verse above and pray the Morning Offering together as a family.

Morning Offering: Dear Lord Jesus, thank you for the gift of today—your Sunday. Please guide our family as we strive to grow closer to you and to one another. Open our hearts and teach us to be more generous with our time. Open our eyes to discover opportunities to love others. Amen.

Pray: *Our Father, Hail Mary, Glory Be.*

REFLECT

Sunday is certainly a day that is meant for worship of our Lord and God and for growing in our Faith. Ponder ways you might grow in Faith, as well as help your family to grow. Consider a few simple, but concrete ideas:

Get everyone to the Sacrament of Reconciliation soon. It's a powerful sacrament that, by cleaning our souls, leads us closer to heaven!

Study the lives of the saints who inspire you to live holy lives. Read short excerpts at the dinner table. The farmer St. Isidore is very fitting, since this Sunday is all about growing the Faith with a teaching about farmers.

Reach out as a family to help someone in need. Doing works of mercy is indeed good for the soul. Put that into practice soon.

CHOOSE AN ACTIVITY

Vegetable garden: One possibility for an activity is to plant a vegetable garden. Draw it out on paper. It might be just simple plant pots on your deck if you lack the space or energy to plant a vegetable garden. Ask the family what they would like to do together. Remember that resting is also an activity—make time for that too! If possible, carve out time to get a bit of exercise as well. Should you choose to plant a vegetable garden or potted plants, have fun choosing seeds or plants the next time you go out, or order some online. You can expand upon your planning throughout the week, being open to ideas and suggestions from the family. Have fun planting the seeds together!

NOTE TO PARENTS AND GRANDPARENTS

Since this is "Growing in Faith Sunday talk" to the family about the importance of growing in their Faith. Explain that the beautiful gift of the virtue of Faith that they received at Baptism is meant to grow throughout their lives. Let them know that they have wonderful and almost endless opportunities throughout their lives to grow and move forward in Faith, rather than stay still and become stagnant. Nourish your family's Faith with solid Church-approved material.

MINI TEACHING

What can we learn from farmers? As Catholics, we know that we are to grow in Faith. That beautiful theological virtue gifted to us at our Baptisms is meant to flourish in our hearts throughout our pilgrimage through life. Consider the hardworking farmers who till the soil and plant seeds for their crops. After the hard work of tilling and tending plants, the farmer must also harvest them at the proper times, being mindful of impending droughts, flooding, or damaging storms. Farmers must ultimately trust the Creator of the universe for the outcome of their labors, because, no matter how technically advanced we might be, the farmer cannot control the weather.

Making our way to heaven is similar to the farmer's work. We must till the soil of our hearts and souls, as well as those for whom we care. Our hearts and souls and theirs must contain "fertile soil" and be "watered" properly. We cannot expect a bountiful and holy "harvest" if our "soil" is not nourished with God's Word and teachings. We must trust God with our lives (Jesus, I trust in You!), just as the farmer must count on God for good weather conditions.

Ponder this simple organic teaching and convey it to the children in your own words. If desired, encourage them to illustrate, with crayons or markers, a farmer growing crops. Throughout the week, be mindful of nourishing the "soil" of the soul with proper "fertilizer."

PONDER

Ponder ways in which you can become more alive in your Faith this springtime, as well as ways to nurture the seeds of Faith in your children's hearts.

FAMILY EVENING PRAYER

to be prayed each evening this week

Dear Lord, thank you for the blessings of this day—your day. If we have failed you in any way, please forgive us. If we have failed one another by not taking care of our responsibilities, please forgive us, Lord. Please help us to grow in holiness each day. Please help us to nourish the "soil" of our souls with your Word and Truth. We love you! Saint Isidore the farmer, please pray for us! Amen.

Pray: *Our Father, Hail Mary, Glory Be.*

CHAPTER 4

Rainy Sunday

"Then he prayed again, and the heaven gave rain and the earth yielded its harvest."
—James 5:18

FAMILY MORNING PRAYER

Read the verse above and pray the Morning Offering together as a family.

Morning Offering: Dear Lord Jesus, thank you for the gift of this Sunday. Please guide our family as we strive to grow closer to you and to one another. Open our hearts and teach us to be much more generous with our time. Open our eyes to discover opportunities to love others. Amen.

Pray: *Our Father, Hail Mary, Glory Be.*

REFLECT

Rainy days can cause us to feel just as dreary as the gray damp weather. Make a strong effort to keep a light and cheerful attitude and help the family do the same. Perhaps you might consider telling silly jokes! Have the kids come up with some. You can try these out since it's not likely that your family will throw tomatoes at you!

What does everyone have on their face? Tu-lips!
"What did the carrot say to the wheat? Lettuce rest, I'm feeling beet."
   —Shel Silverstein
How do you stop critters from digging in your garden?
   Take away their shovels!
Knock, knock! Who's there? Lettuce. Lettuce who?
   Lettuce in, it's cold out here!
Why did the rabbit cross the garden? To get to the other side?

No, because the lettuce was greener there!
Why didn't anyone laugh at the garden jokes?
They were too "corn-ey"!

Consider your own ideas to keep a happy spirit today. Try to smile often—it's contagious!

CHOOSE AN ACTIVITY

Since it's a rainy day, here are activity suggestions:

Fun rainy-day activity: Today at breakfast, after Grace Before Meals, ask the kids which board game they'd like to play together. It's a wonderful thing to pause from routine and make the time to play together. Sunday is the perfect day! If the sun happens to surprise you and comes out later, go on out in the fresh air.

Congo line: In keeping with the growing plants theme, get together in a "Congo line" and do a funny marching dance from room to room in your home. Stop in each room and observe the plant life (or lack thereof). Have the kids count how many plants are in your home. Talk to them about taking care of the life that God gifts to us.

Planting seeds: It's rewarding and even educational watching plants grow! Gather the family and your art supplies to decorate flowerpots with markers, paints, or crayons. You will need a few packages of flower or vegetable seeds, potting soil, and a few small terra cotta or other types of flowerpots in advance. You can use disposable paper drink cups, as well. Fill three decorated flowerpots about three-quarters full with potting soil, and plant the desired flower or vegetable seeds in the pots. Water the seeds, and place the pots in a sunny window. Water the seeds about two or three times a week. One flower pot can be used as a gift for someone, another can be used on a prayer table in your home in honor of the Blessed Mother (especially if you are in the month of May), and the third can be placed somewhere in your home.

NOTE TO PARENTS AND GRANDPARENTS

Talk to the children about sowing and reaping at the dinner table tonight. You can begin with this verse: "The point is this: the one who sows sparingly will also reap sparingly, and the one who sows bountifully will also reap bountifully" (2 Cor. 9:6). Ask family members to weigh in on what this might mean to them, and enjoy a nice discussion. As always, be sure to set parameters regarding technology use for today—how much you will allow the kids to engage in. Perhaps your family can step away from the internet, video games, social media, and television completely today to better experience one another's presence and listen to God speaking to your hearts in a greater way. Push beyond your comfort zone to try it!

MINI TEACHING

Spending time as a family is not only wonderful; it is many times educational as well. Consider that we breathe in and out about twelve to fourteen times per minute, usually without thought. Tell the children that we should thank God even for our breathing that we take for granted. After all, it keeps us alive! For a bit of education today, you might consider telling the kids that houseplants improve air quality (if they are mature enough to grasp this). If possible, in the coming week read about the plants that NASA recommends for air quality in this article: http://www.mnn.com/health/healthy-spaces/stories/best-air-filtering-houseplants-according-to-nasa, or do your own research and create a teachable moment from observing your houseplants. You might even seize this opportunity to explain that smoking is very detrimental to one's health.

Ponder ways in which you can become more alive in your Faith this springtime. Nurture those seeds of Faith in the children's hearts! You might find yourself out and about more often now that the better weather is here. Your Christian example to your family and others can be transforming to others in this beautiful season of hope.

FAMILY EVENING PRAYER
to be prayed each evening this week

Dear Lord, thank you for being with us this day—your day. If we have failed to grow in holiness, forgive us, please. If we have failed one another by not responding with love, forgive us, Lord. We love you and we want to come closer to you still. Thank you for your many blessings! Amen.

Pray: *Our Father, Hail Mary, Glory Be.*

PART TWO

Summer Sundays

"A child who gathers in summer is prudent, but a child who sleeps in harvest brings shame."
—Proverbs 10:5

In this season of summer, strive to find more times to sit at the dinner table together as a family. It is there where you can share with one another and even grow in your Faith. I'd like to share a story about a seemingly homeless little girl that Mother Teresa took in and cared for. I'll start by saying that the dinner table is a place of community, no matter the family size or setting.

Mother Teresa found a little girl on the streets of Calcutta. The saint of the gutters took her into the safety of the convent. After a few days, the girl went missing. The Sisters later discovered her under a tree—her family's home without walls. The child left the convent's security, returning to the comforting community of her family—eating meagerly, but all together in love under the branches of a tree.

Ponder ways in which you can become more alive in your faith together with your family this summertime. Many opportunities will unfold in which your Christian example to your family and others can help uplift spirits in this bright and happy summer season.

CHAPTER 5

Summer Fun Sunday

"God's action is the model for human action. If God 'rested and was refreshed' on the seventh day, man too ought to 'rest' and should let others, especially the poor, 'be refreshed.'"
—Catechism of the Catholic Church, no. 2172

FAMILY MORNING PRAYER

Read the verse above and pray the Morning Offering together as a family.

Morning Offering: Dear Lord Jesus, thank you for the gift of today—your day. Please guide our family as we strive to grow closer to you and to one another. Open our hearts and teach us to be much more generous with our time. Open our eyes to discover opportunities to love others. Amen.

Pray: *Our Father, Hail Mary, Glory Be.*

REFLECT

Strive to spend more time together as a family this summertime, especially on Sundays. You can do so very naturally when breaking bread together. Eating together can be therapeutic and healing. Many countries treat mealtimes as sacred, lingering over meals and sharing meaningful conversations with loved ones. Yet, sadly, the average American family consumes far too much fast food, and doesn't eat together regularly.

Eating is necessary for survival, but enjoying a meal together is transformative. We should avoid hurried eating or while working at computers or on our electronic devices. We'd be wise to relearn the art of lingering family dinners and heart-to heart conversations. Granted, we are not living in the time of *Leave It to Beaver* or *Father Knows Best*, and perhaps we fear that we lack the luxury of time required to cook a decent meal. Yet, "breaking bread" together and sharing hearts doesn't have to be complicated to provide tremendous benefits! Try to unplug for your family. Spend more time listening to and enjoying one another's company instead of being a slave to your devices.

CHOOSE AN ACTIVITY

Make a meal together: Since we are discussing spending time as a family when "breaking bread" together, perhaps you will make a meal together. I suggest that you don't expect perfection in the kitchen or at the dinner table. Also, you can expect a bit of a mess when working together in the kitchen. Try not to worry. You are creating wonderful experiences and memories.

Invent a board game: Since today is "Summer Fun Sunday," in addition to cooking together, you might decide to do something fun that you've never done before or even sit down and invent a board game together! Yes, I said, "Invent." Be creative! Resting is also an activity! Even God rested as we read in the verse at the beginning of today's reflections. Strive to carve out a time to rest and refresh.

NOTE TO PARENTS AND GRANDPARENTS

Talk to the children about the need to get rest and also be refreshed on Sunday—the Lord's Day. Read today's verse again from the Catechism. Tell them that when you make plans for Sundays, it should always include some rest. You might find a bit of rest by doing one or more of the following:

> Take a nap.
> Don't plan too much activity.
> Carve out time to sit and relax.
> Close your eyes for ten or fifteen minutes and breathe deeply.
> Take time to read, ponder, and pray.
> Cut down on technology use.
> Make time for conversations with other family members.

MINI TEACHING

If our Lord and Savior rested when he was creating the universe, shouldn't we take a cue from him? The Catechism teaches: "By a tradition handed down from the apostles which took its origin from the very day of Christ's Resurrection, the Church celebrates the Paschal mystery every seventh day, which day is appropriately called the Lord's Day or Sunday." The day of Christ's Resurrection is both the first day of the week, the memorial of the first day of creation, and the "eighth day," on which Christ after his "rest" on the great Sabbath inaugurates the "day that the Lord has made," the "day that knows no evening" (CCC, no. 1166).

PONDER

Ponder ways in which you can become more alive in your Faith this summer. When you are out and about in the summer weather, you will hopefully discover new opportunities to engage with others. Strive to be an exemplary Christian example to your family and others in this marvelous summer season. As well, have fun! Make the time to laugh and be happy! Your family will love you for it!

FAMILY EVENING PRAYER

to be prayed each evening this week

Dear Lord, thank you for the blessings of this day—your day. If we have failed you in any way, please forgive us. If we have failed one another by not taking care of our responsibilities, please forgive us, Lord. Please help us to grow in holiness each day. Help us to observe Sundays with more reverence. We love you, Jesus! Amen.

Pray: *Our Father, Hail Mary, Glory Be.*

CHAPTER 6

Sun-sational Sunday

"Love is patient; love is kind; love is not envious or boastful or arrogant or rude. It does not insist on its own way; it is not irritable or resentful; it does not rejoice in wrongdoing, but rejoices in the truth. It bears all things, believes all things, hopes all things, endures all things."
—1 Corinthians 13:4–7

FAMILY MORNING PRAYER

Read the verse above and pray the Morning Offering together as a family.

Morning Offering: Dear Lord Jesus, thank you for the gift of today—your Sunday. Please guide our family as we strive to grow closer to you and to one another. Open our hearts and teach us to be much more generous with our time. Open our eyes to discover opportunities to love others. Amen.

Pray: *Our Father, Hail Mary, Glory Be.*

REFLECT

Throughout this book, I discuss the goal of working at spending more family meals together. I'd like to underscore the fact that regular family dinners make a huge difference in everybody's lives. Let's take a quick look at physical and psychological implications of families eating together. First of all, home-cooked meals are usually healthier than fast food. Additionally, eating together provides an opportunity to be with loved ones, destress, catch up on each person's news, enjoy meaningful conversation, improve family relationships, and pray and learn more about the Faith together.

Studies show that children who eat with their families five times a week or more are far less prone to abuse alcohol or drugs, or become smokers. Academically, they achieve higher and report feeling closer to their parents than do children who eat less often with their parents. Certainly, this gives us much to ponder.

CHOOSE AN ACTIVITY

Since this is "Sun-sational Sunday," think of ways that you can let your light and love shine to others.

Create Encouraging Greeting Cards: Your family can create loving handmade greeting cards that can be gifted anonymously to folks you know who might need encouragement. Gather the family and the art supplies and have fun! You don't need to be an artist!

Happy Sunshine Craft: Using yellow paper plates or white plates painted or colored yellow, craft a happy sunshine face. Then, on yellow construction paper, trace around the children's hands, making enough to go around the plate and cut them out. Affix the paper hands all around the back of the paper plate so that the fingers of the hand cutouts look like the sun's rays. The children can draw smiling faces on the sunshine. Let the children decide to whom they will give their sunshine. With your help, on each creation write a note that answers this question: "What makes you shine like the sun?" This craft will give the children the opportunity to be happy givers while also complimenting the recipient of the gift by letting them know that they shine like the sun in some way (which will be noted on the sunshine)!

NOTE TO PARENTS AND GRANDPARENTS

Talk to the children about being more loving to others. Read again today's verse from 1 Corinthians. Strive to be more cognizant about your tone of voice and mannerisms. Consider whether or not they convey God's love. Why or why not? Ask the children to think about this, as well. Find time to rest; recharging your "batteries" by resting makes for a happier family!

MINI TEACHING

In his encyclical *The Gospel of Life,* St. John Paul II called the family the sanctuary of life. He stated, "Within the family each member is accepted, respected, and honored precisely because he or she is a person; and if any family member is in greater need, the care which she or he receives is all the more intense and attentive."[2]

Think about how your family accepts, respects, and honors one another. Is there room for improvement? There should be! There always will be, so don't be discouraged. After all, we are all works in progress and we are not in heaven yet! Encourage the family to be more loving to one another and to everyone they meet. Ask them to tell you three ways in which they can do just that.

PONDER

Ponder ways in which you can become more alive in your Faith this summer. Make efforts to move beyond your comfort zone in reaching out with Christ's love to others. As you pray, allow God to heal you of hurts and make you new so that you will be an exemplary Christian example to your family and others in this marvelous season of warmth and happiness.

Have fun with the family. Don't take yourself too seriously! Yes, life is serious, but make room for playing and laughing! You are creating sweet memories together.

FAMILY EVENING PRAYER

to be prayed each evening this week

Dear Lord, thank you for the blessings of this day—your day. If we have failed you in any way, please forgive us. If we have failed one another by not taking care of our responsibilities, please forgive us, Lord. Please help us to grow in holiness each day. We love you! Amen.

Pray: *Our Father, Hail Mary, Glory Be.*

✐ CHAPTER 7 ✐

Barefoot Sunday

"Hear, O Israel: The LORD is our God, the LORD alone. You shall love the LORD your God with all your heart, and with all your soul, and with all your might. Keep these words that I am commanding you today in your heart. Recite them to your children and talk about them when you are at home and when you are away, when you lie down and when you rise. Bind them as a sign on your hand, fix them as an emblem on your forehead, and write them on the doorposts of your house and on your gates."
—Deuteronomy 6:4–9

FAMILY MORNING PRAYER

Read the verse above and pray the Morning Offering together as a family.

Morning Offering: Dear Lord Jesus, thank you for the gift of today—your Sunday. Please guide our family as we strive to grow closer to you and to one another. Open our hearts and teach us to be much more generous with our time. Open our eyes to discover opportunities to love others. Amen.

Pray: *Our Father, Hail Mary, Glory Be.*

REFLECT

After reading today's verse, take time to ponder the meaning. How might you "Love the LORD your God with all your heart, and with all your soul, and with all your might"? How might this be accomplished in the family? Ask everyone their thoughts.

CHOOSE AN ACTIVITY

Footprints on paper or in sand: If you're feeling courageous, perhaps you might do a craft that involves painting the bottoms of your children's feet and having them make foot images on a big piece of butcher paper or empty newsprint spread across the floor or outside on the driveway. When the paint dries, add the date and the children's names and ages beside their footprints. With markers or crayons, add inspiring traditional or original verses about walking in Faith. You could also paste a copy of the poem "Footprints" (see below in the Mini Teaching section) to your creation. If you do this outside on a warm summer day, washing their feet can be fun, too, as they dip them in a pan of sudsy water and you help them rinse off their feet with a watering can! If you'd rather not use paint, instead trace around your children's feet with markers or crayons. Have the children fill their "feet" in with colorful markers or crayons.

Hang your masterpiece on a clothes line, a bulletin board, or wherever desired. Later, fold it up and store it away in a memory box for reminiscing in years to come. The children will marvel about the sizes of their feet way back when! I suspect that you will too!

At the beach: If you go to the beach, make fun footprints in the sand and take pictures of them. Use the photos to create a mural similar to the idea above.

Have a picnic: If not outside, or at the beach, then on a blanket on your living room floor! While you're at it, read a story to the family. Be sure to fit in moments of rest and refreshment today.

NOTE TO PARENTS AND GRANDPARENTS

Talk to the children about the need to love God with all their hearts, souls, and with all their might. Ask them if they endeavor to do so. Have them list at least three ways in which they do, as well as three ways that they could try harder.

MINI TEACHING

Read the following poem to the family.

Footprints

One night I dreamed a dream.
As I was walking along the beach with my Lord.
Across the dark sky flashed scenes from my life.
For each scene, I noticed two sets of footprints in the sand,
One belonging to me and one to my Lord.
After the last scene of my life flashed before me,
I looked back at the footprints in the sand.
I noticed that at many times along the path of my life,
especially at the very lowest and saddest times,
there was only one set of footprints.
This really troubled me, so I asked the Lord about it.
"Lord, you said once I decided to follow you,
You'd walk with me all the way.
But I noticed that during the saddest and most troublesome times of my life,
there was only one set of footprints.
I don't understand why, when I needed You the most, You would leave me."
He whispered, "My precious child, I love you and will never leave you
Never, ever, during your trials and testings.
When you saw only one set of footprints,
It was then that I carried you."
—Author unknown

Ask each family member to comment on the poem in their own way. Take the opportunity to tell the family that while this is just a poem, we can be assured that God loves us very much and indeed "carries" us throughout the challenging parts of our lives. He will grant us many graces and blessings, and he desires that we pray to him and ask for his help.

Perhaps the children will think of someone they know who is enduring a trial or might feel all alone. Think of ways to help that person, reminding the family that smiles and kindness indeed go a long way.

PONDER

Consider ways in which you can become more alive in your Faith. Have fun with the family in this stunning season of warmth and happiness. Make room for playing and laughing to create beautiful experiences and memories.

FAMILY EVENING PRAYER

to be prayed each evening this week

Dear Lord, thank you for the blessings of this day—your day. If we have failed you in any way, please forgive us. If we have failed one another by not taking care of our responsibilities, please forgive us, Lord. Please help us to grow in holiness each day. We love you! Amen.

Pray: *Our Father, Hail Mary, Glory Be.*

All Abloom Sunday

"They are like trees planted by streams of water, which yield their fruit in its season, and their leaves do not wither. In all that they do, they prosper. The wicked are not so, but are like chaff that the wind drives away. Therefore the wicked will not stand in the judgment, nor sinners in the congregation of the righteous."
—Psalm 1:3–5

FAMILY MORNING PRAYER

Read the verse above and pray the Morning Offering together as a family.

Morning Offering: Dear Lord Jesus, thank you for the gift of today—your Sunday. Please guide our family as we strive to grow closer to you and to one another. Open our hearts and teach us to be much more generous with our time. Open our eyes to discover opportunities to love others. Amen.

Pray: *Our Father, Hail Mary, Glory Be.*

REFLECT

We are familiar with the saying "Bloom where you are planted." Popularized by artist Mary Englebreit, we see it on just about everything from teacups, tee shirts, to wall murals. It has been attributed to St. Francis de Sales (1567–1622). Specifically, the saint expressed, "Truly charity has no limit; for the love of God has been poured into our hearts by His Spirit dwelling in each one of us, calling us to a life of devotion and inviting us to bloom in the garden where He has planted and directing us to radiate the beauty and spread the fragrance of His Providence." What does this mean to you? What could it mean to your family? Can you "bloom" right where you are?

CHOOSE AN ACTIVITY

Since we are discussing "blooming," why not consider a craft or project that relates to growing? As well, ask the family what they would like to do together. Remember that resting is also an activity!

Garden art box: Many artists go out into the garden for inspiration. Help the children (your budding artists) to create a garden art box. Transform an empty shoebox into a great place to keep their art supplies. Use old seed catalogues or pictures of flowers from magazines to decorate the outside of the box. Fill the box with crayons, pencils, chalk, a pad of paper, and whatever items you decide upon.

Pressed flowers: Enjoy time together by going on a plant and flower expedition! Collect leaves and flowers that you will press and preserve. You'll need to supervise so that poisonous plants will not be collected inadvertently. You don't need a flower press. Squares of corrugated cardboard and pieces of plywood boards cut to the same size will work. Newspaper or blotter paper will go inside the cardboard. Collect fresh flowers, and place them between the newspaper or blotter paper, which will be between the cardboard (which allows air movement during the drying process). When you have placed the plants as you like them, apply the wooden boards on either side and put a strong rubber band or bungie cord around it all. Place books or a weight on the stack for pressure. The plants will usually dry in about two weeks, with some plants taking a bit longer. Once they have dried, use your imagination as to how you will use the dried flowers. You might want to use a glue like "Mod Podge" to decorate the outside of a wooden box or your "garden art box"! Perhaps the pressed flowers will decorate the cover of a notebook. As well, you can glue them to a stiff paper and frame your masterpiece! No doubt, you'll enjoy God's beautiful creation when you gaze upon your finished project.

NOTE TO PARENTS AND GRANDPARENTS

Talk to the children about the notion of "blooming" where they are "planted." Suggest ways that they can grow and thrive in God's garden with God's abiding love. However, we want to impress upon our families that we don't stop there. We can't simply bask in God's love for us. We must share it! Ponder a loving work of mercy that you can do with your family in the very near future. Talk to them about it and ask their ideas.

Can you help? Is there someone nearby, an elderly neighbor perhaps, who needs help? Can you make a homemade meal and take it to them? Possibly, you can offer to help with yard work. Even a phone call to let someone know that you care can be quite beneficial.

MINI TEACHING

It's not necessarily something you might be thinking about each ordinary day. However, a Catholic home is meant to become a *domestic church*. It is where the children first learn about God. According to the Second Vatican Council's Dogmatic Constitution on the Church: "The family, is so to speak, the domestic church."
—Papal encyclical *Lumen Gentium*, no. 11

It's important to ponder that if you are not keeping a watchful eye on your domestic church, problems can occur. I should say that problems *will* occur. The bad influence of the culture will creep in. It's paramount for Catholic parents, grandparents, and caregivers to ensure that God is the Master of the home.

We begin "building" our domestic church through a life of family prayer and love. Your typical day at home in the family might not always mirror a page out of *Butler's Lives of the Saints*. Probably far from it, most times! However, Catholic families truly work out their salvation within the walls of their domestic church. The key word here is "work"! We must work at it and always do our best to draw our families closer to God through our prayerful example and continual teachings within our domestic church. It's our foremost job, after all. Throughout this book,

I give suggestions for keeping your domestic church holy. You can also refer to the back of the book to get some additional ideas.

PONDER

Ponder ways in which you and your family can become more alive in your Faith this summer. Carve out time to pray together, which is very essential in the building of your domestic church. As you pray, ask God to heal your hearts of any hurts and allow God to make you new. You and your family can be exemplary Christian examples to others in this sweet season of warmth and happiness.

FAMILY EVENING PRAYER
to be prayed each evening this week

Dear Lord, thank you for the blessings of this day—your day. If we have failed you in any way, please forgive us. If we have failed one another by not taking care of our responsibilities, please forgive us, Lord. Please help us to grow in holiness each day. We love you! Amen.

Pray: *Our Father, Hail Mary, Glory Be.*

Autumn Sundays

"They answered, 'Believe on the Lord Jesus, and you will be saved, you and your household.'"
—Acts 16:31

W here I live in the Northeast, the stunning season of autumn brings about big changes. We can expect the swift unfolding of color as hot summer air turns cooler. The once-luscious green leaves of trees and plants suddenly take on blazing colors of reds, burnt orange, and yellow. For a time, everything seems all ablaze with vibrant color. Folks often travel to these parts to see autumn shine forth in all its glory.

As the hot summer temperatures flee, the encroaching, invigorating cooler temperatures rush in and cause the once-brilliant leaves to turn brittle and fall to the ground—to be crushed under feet and vehicles. I then become acutely aware that the frigid season of winter is just around the corner and realize that it would be wise to get outside to stretch my legs and enjoy the crisp days of autumn. As well, I have to prepare for the upcoming freezing season of winter. I do have to be careful on my hikes because wildlife such as wolves and black bears live in my neck of the woods.

What can we learn in the season of autumn? As we prepare for winter ahead, can we also spiritually prepare our hearts? I believe that we can and should.

All Ablaze Sunday

"Grandchildren are the crown of the aged, and the glory of children is their parents."
—Proverbs 17:6

FAMILY MORNING PRAYER

Read the verse above and pray the Morning Offering together as a family.

Morning Offering: Dear Lord Jesus, thank you for the gift of today—your Sunday. Please guide our family as we strive to grow closer to you and to one another. Open our hearts and teach us to be much more generous with our time. Open our eyes to discover opportunities to love others. Amen.

Pray: *Our Father, Hail Mary, Glory Be.*

REFLECT

In today's verse we hear about grandchildren as an integral part of the family. I have fond memories of my grandmother, my mother's mother. She was the only grandparent I knew, because the others had passed on before I was born. Yet, the love that she poured out and the seeds of Faith that she planted in my heart made a lasting impression on my little heart as a child, and they continue to do so now that I am a mother and grandmother myself. Grandparents' love and prayers for their family are powerful. Let's be sure to reach out to grandparents often. If there are none in your life, consider "adopting" one!

CHOOSE AN ACTIVITY

You might decide upon a craft or activity that involves grandparents.

Cards and visits: The children can make homemade greeting cards to send to their grandparent or possibly an elderly person they know from the neighborhood or parish. A heartfelt greeting can go a long way in lifting someone's spirits. Consider calling, visiting, or planning a visit to a grandparent or an elderly relative soon.

Make a special meal or dessert together: Make a meal or dessert using a grandparent's recipe. You might have it handy in your recipe box or notebook. However, calling or visiting a grandparent to ask about their recipes will indeed make them happy. It's truly a "win-win" situation. You'll also be carrying down traditions from your family's past and possibly creating new customs with your children and grandchildren. It's so important to stay in touch with our families. It is within the family that we can relish in a beautiful gift and sense of belonging that gives us strength to carry on.

NOTE TO PARENTS AND GRANDPARENTS

Talk to the children about grandparents. If their grandparents have passed away, try your best to tell the children a story about them. It's important to "dust off" those "pages" of history and pass them down to the youngsters. If you are not certain of your family's history, make a point to find out more about it soon by getting in touch with older relatives, if possible.

MINI TEACHING
for parents, grandparents, and caregivers

The Church teaches that the family is the basic cell of society. We find our identity in the family. We can feel a sense of belonging. It's essential to raise our children and grandchildren in a loving family.

Saint John Paul II stated in his Apostolic Exhortation *Familiaris Consortio,* "The family, which is founded and given life by love, is a community of persons: of husband and wife, of parents and children, of relatives. Its first task is to live with fidelity the reality of communion in a constant effort to develop an authentic community of persons." The former pontiff goes on to tell us what power and goal drives us to live in this communion of persons. It is love! He wrote, "The inner principle of that task, its permanent power and its final goal is love: without love the family is not a community of persons and, in the same way, without love the family cannot live, grow and perfect itself as a community of persons." He then explained how mankind cannot love without love.

Specifically, he wrote, "What I wrote in the Encyclical Redemptor hominis applies primarily and especially within the family as such: 'Man cannot live without love. He remains a being that is incomprehensible for himself, his life is senseless, if love is not revealed to him, if he does not encounter love, if he does not experience it and make it his own, if he does not participate intimately in it.'"[3]

Think about the love of a family and the numerous times that forgiveness and tenderness come into play. We must lovingly bear with one another with patience to grow in holiness. We can look to the Holy Family as an exemplary model for authentic love.

PONDER

Ponder ways in which you and your family can become more alive in your Faith during this season of autumn. Consider St. John Paul II's words, that your "first task is to live with fidelity the reality of communion in a constant effort to develop an authentic community of persons." The family is so important! Strive to create your own family traditions as you also mirror the traditions of holy Mother Church. Don't forget to smile and have fun with the family too. Make room for playing and laughing. You are creating marvelous experiences and memories for your family.

FAMILY EVENING PRAYER
to be prayed each evening this week

Dear Lord, thank you for the blessings of this day—your day. If we have failed you in any way, please forgive us. If we have failed one another by not taking care of our responsibilities, please forgive us, Lord. Please help us to grow in holiness each day. We love you! Amen.

Pray: *Our Father, Hail Mary, Glory Be.*

CHAPTER 10

Pumpkin and Spice Sunday

"Sons are indeed a heritage from the Lord, the fruit of the womb a reward. Like arrows in the hand of a warrior are the sons of one's youth. Happy is the man who has his quiver full of them. He shall not be put to shame when he speaks with his enemies in the gate."
—Psalm 127:3–5

FAMILY MORNING PRAYER

Read the verse above and pray the Morning Offering together as a family.

Morning Offering: Dear Lord Jesus, thank you for the gift of today—your Sunday. Please guide our family as we strive to grow closer to you and to one another. Open our hearts and teach us to be much more generous with our time. Open our eyes to discover opportunities to love others. Amen.

Pray: *Our Father, Hail Mary, Glory Be.*

REFLECT

In this season of autumn, we have a chapter entitled, "Pumpkin and Spice Sunday." Those words might conjure up ideas of baking (and eating!) delicious cinnamon-y muffins, sipping pumpkin-spiced hot drinks, or maybe even curling up someplace under a warm blanket with a good book! Maybe it will be a cookbook and you can get ideas for future Sunday dinners!

The word *pumpkin* also brings memories to me of bumpy rides through the pumpkin patch with my children. Each autumn, we made a point to visit a local pumpkin patch where we made our way through rows and rows of all sizes of orange-colored pumpkins, while sitting in between bales of scratchy hay on a tractor-drawn cart.

Our verse today speaks of children as the fruit and rewards of our wombs. Be sure to relish in the gift of family—whether you have one child or grandchild, or a full "quiver" of them. Every child is a gift. Every family is a blessing. Worship, play, rest, serve, and together work out your salvation today on the Lord's Day. Have fun!

CHOOSE AN ACTIVITY

Do you want to bake healthy, but tasty muffins? You can make extra and gift them to someone.

Recipes: Peruse recipes online or in cookbooks. I highly encourage using family recipes. You can even change them up a bit to add your own flair. As well, ask the family what they would like to do together. Remember that resting is also an activity! Make time for a short respite to close your eyes and breathe deeply.

Healthy Pumpkin Muffin Recipe

Ingredients

3 cups old-fashioned oats (or 8 and a half ounces oat flour)

1 tablespoon pumpkin pie spice (or combination of cinnamon, ground ginger, ground allspice, ground cloves, and ground nutmeg)

1 1/2 teaspoons baking soda

3/4 teaspoon fine sea salt

2 eggs

1 cup milk or unsweetened almond milk (plain or vanilla)

1 cup pumpkin puree (from can, preferably organic)

1/2 cup pure maple syrup (or honey)

3 tablespoons melted coconut oil (or mild-flavored oil)

1 teaspoon vanilla extract

Directions

Preheat oven to 375° F. Lightly grease muffin tins with cooking spray. Set aside.

Puree the oats in a blender or food processor to a flour-like consistency.

Add in all dry ingredients (pumpkin pie spice, baking soda and sea salt). Pulse mixture to combine evenly. Set aside.

In a separate large mixing bowl, whisk together the eggs, milk, pumpkin puree, pure maple syrup (or honey), oil, and vanilla extract until evenly combined.

Fold the dry ingredients in with the wet ingredient mixture.

Stir until the mixture is just combined. Avoid overmixing.

Portion the ingredients into prepared muffin tins.

Bake for 15–18 minutes, or until a toothpick inserted into the center of the muffins comes out clean.

Remove pan from the oven and place on a cooling rack for 5 minutes.

Serve muffins warm (with butter if desired) or let the muffins cool to room temperature and store in a sealed container for up to 3 days (preferably in refrigerator), or freeze for up to 3 months.

Enjoy!

NOTE TO PARENTS AND GRANDPARENTS

Talk to the children about the need to get rest and also be refreshed on Sunday—the Lord's Day. Every Sunday should have even a short period of rest. We need to recharge our "batteries," after all. Try to incorporate a short period of rest for everyone, unplugged from unnecessary technology.

MINI TEACHING

It's essential to have regular meal times together as a family. No doubt, it's not always possible to be together at every meal due to busy schedules and other factors. However, as Catholic parents and grandparents, we need to do our best to make these together times occur more often than not. Make a huge effort to be together for Sunday dinners. Here are five tips for making dinner happen and making it happy:

1) Plan ahead: don't try to throw dinner together at the last minute.

2 Keep it simple: but make it healthy.

3 Get kids involved: helping set the table, cooking, and cleaning up.

4) Be flexible: don't expect perfect behavior. Preserve harmony and peace at the dinner table.

5) Make it special, especially on Sundays: light a candle, add fresh flowers to the table, invite our Lord as your guest! Pray together as a family!

Meaningful memories are created each time you gather together to eat. You show family your love by planning dinner and eating together. That said, get the kids involved in planning a meal together! Encourage them to share something meaningful (news or something they've learned) at each dinner. It's a good way to make conversations happen.

PONDER

Ponder ways in which you can become more alive in your Faith, not only on Sundays. Take time to plan special upcoming Sunday dinners. Don't forget to have fun with the family. Smile, play and laugh! You will be happy that you took the time to slow down and enjoy the family.

FAMILY EVENING PRAYER

to be prayed each evening this week

Dear Lord, thank you for the blessings of this day—your day. If we have failed you in any way, please forgive us. If we have failed one another by not taking care of our responsibilities, please forgive us, Lord. Please help us to grow in holiness each day. We love you! Amen.

Pray: *Our Father, Hail Mary, Glory Be.*

CHAPTER 11

Bountiful Sunday

"Train children in the right way, and when old, they will not stray."
—Proverbs 22:6

FAMILY MORNING PRAYER

Read the verse above and pray the Morning Offering together as a family.

Morning Offering: Dear Lord Jesus, thank you for the gift of today—
your Sunday. Please guide our family as we strive to grow closer to you
and to one another. Open our hearts and teach us to be much more
generous with our time. Open our eyes to discover opportunities to love
others. Amen.

Pray: *Our Father, Hail Mary, Glory Be.*

REFLECT

Our opening verse speaks about teaching children well and how those
valuable teachings will stay with them throughout life. As parents and
grandparents, we must do our best to really be there for children as
their first and foremost educators, as the Church instructs. We absolutely
cannot get lazy and allow (even inadvertently) the culture to teach the little
ones or to influence us to let down our guard. In teaching our children
about living virtuous lives, we can take a tip from St. Basil, bishop of
Caesarea (AD 339–379), who said, "A good deed is never lost; he who sows
courtesy reaps friendship, and he who plants kindness gathers love." His
sage advice was not just for ancient times. Rather, it is very relevant today.
Our children need to show common courtesy to others, but also to move
a bit beyond their comfort zones to show Christ's love to others.

Speak with the children about being courteous and respectful. Ask
them to list three ways in which they can show more courtesy to others.

While we are at it, how about we change the response "No problem!" that we often hear when we say, "Thank you"? Let's reclaim the phrase "You are welcome!" Hopefully, with our sincere efforts, it will catch on!

CHOOSE AN ACTIVITY

Apple picking: Every year when the weather starts to turn a little crisp here in the Northeast, I get a hankering to go apple picking with the family. I love to experience the smells and sights of the apple orchard with my family. We pick a variety of apples and bring them home to make hot apple crisp or apple pie. Even though my kids are grown and my oldest daughter has children herself, if they can arrange their schedule, some of my kids come home for a visit this time of year specifically for an apple orchard outing. We love it! I guess we can say that we have established this fun family tradition.

Perhaps you can visit a local apple orchard. Be sure to snap photos! I have no doubt that you'll enjoy the confections you make with your family, the cinnamon-y smells wafting through your kitchen, as well as the pure delight in simply eating fresh juicy apples right from the tree. I must confess—my mouth is watering as I write this!

Healthy and Delicious Apple Crisp Recipe

Serves six

(I usually double or triple this recipe to have enough to share)

Preheat oven to 375° F.

Prepare the crumb topping.

In a medium bowl combine the crumb-topping ingredients with a pastry blender or fork until the mixture resembles small crumbs. Refrigerate and prepare the apple filling.

Ingredients

For the crumb topping

    1/2 cup brown rice flour or oat flour (or all-purpose flour)

    1/2 cup old-fashioned rolled oats

    1/2 cup honey

1/2 teaspoon baking powder

1/4 teaspoon ground cinnamon (use a high-quality cinnamon for better flavor)

Dash of salt

1/3 cup unsalted butter (cut into small pieces)

For the apple filling

3–4 large Granny Smith or tart baking apples (peeled and sliced thin)

3 tablespoons butter (melted)

2 tablespoons brown rice flour or oat flour (or all-purpose flour)

1 tablespoon lemon juice

3 tablespoons milk

1/2 teaspoon vanilla extract

1/4 cup honey

1/2 teaspoon ground cinnamon

Dash of salt

Directions

Prepare apple filling.

Peel and slice apples.

In a small bowl, combine melted butter and flour until well blended. Add lemon juice, milk, and vanilla and stir well. Stir in honey, cinnamon, and salt.

Pour butter mixture over apples and toss to coat. Pour apple mixture into an 8 x 8-inch baking dish and spread into an even layer.

Sprinkle crumb topping evenly over the apples.

Bake for 30–35 minutes or until golden brown and top is set.

Remove from oven and allow to cool for at least 10 minutes before serving. May be served warm with vanilla ice cream on top!

NOTE TO PARENTS AND GRANDPARENTS

Talk to the children about family togetherness on Sundays. Let them know that you value their presence and that you delight in their contributions and conversations. They should strive to be home on Sundays whenever possible. It's a special day to enjoy together.

MINI TEACHING

Today we focus a bit on learning to be virtuous. In addition to that teaching, encourage the children to share with others. Our title and theme is "Bountiful Sunday." We think of a bountiful harvest at this time of year. We can consider a couple of verses from the Bible: "What shall I return to the LORD for all his bounty to me?" (Ps. 116:12), as well as, "Those who are generous are blessed, for they share their bread with the poor" (Prov. 22:9). Ask the children about this. How can we share our "bounty"? Encourage them to tell you three ways. Write them down. Perhaps you will go apple picking and make an apple recipe that you can share with a shut-in, an elderly neighbor, or someone who would delight in such a treat.

PONDER

Consider ways in which you can become more alive in your Faith. Be sure to teach the family some healthy "prayer habits." When you establish a routine for prayers, it will become a healthy habit! Remember to smile! Don't take yourself too seriously! Make room for playing and laughing! You will be teaching valuable lessons. Seize the Sunday opportunity!

FAMILY EVENING PRAYER

to be prayed each evening this week

Dear Lord, thank you for the blessings of this day—your day. If we have failed you in any way, please forgive us. If we have failed one another by not taking care of our responsibilities, please forgive us, Lord. Please help us to grow in holiness each day. We love you! Amen.

Pray: *Our Father, Hail Mary, Glory Be.*

CHAPTER 12

Harvested Sunday

"In order that rest may not degenerate into emptiness or boredom, it must offer spiritual enrichment, greater freedom, opportunities for contemplation and fraternal communion. Therefore, among the forms of culture and entertainment which society offers, the faithful should choose those which are most in keeping with a life lived in obedience to the precepts of the gospel."
—Saint John Paul II[4]

FAMILY MORNING PRAYER

Read the verse above and pray the Morning Offering together as a family.

Morning Offering: Dear Lord Jesus, thank you for the gift of today—your Sunday. Please guide our family as we strive to grow closer to you and to one another. Open our hearts and teach us to be much more generous with our time. Open our eyes to discover opportunities to love others. Amen.

Pray: *Our Father, Hail Mary, Glory Be.*

REFLECT

Saint John Paul II gives us much food for thought. Have we let our guard down or become too lax in allowing the bad parts of the culture to infiltrate our homes? Are we sure to choose for our family those forms of entertainment that aid us to live in "obedience to the precepts of the gospel"? In addition, think about what ways you can incorporate "spiritual enrichment" into your family's life. Are you "harvesting" fruits and values from your Faith to pass down to the children?

Take a moment to consider your previous choices with regard to what you have allowed for the children and what is not permitted. Take any necessary steps to improve. Write them down. Make it happen! We must keep in mind that parents and grandparents are not always popular with their children because of the healthy and holy parameters that we put into place. Nevertheless, if we do not protect them, who will?

CHOOSE AN ACTIVITY

Create a sacred outside space: Though you might have a dedicated space in your home that serves as a prayer corner or prayer nook, this time of year is perfect to create a sacred space outside in your yard or garden. My good friends Andy and Lisa Andrus have created outdoor Stations of the Cross in their Louisiana backyard. They certainly inspire their large family to pray often and to be mindful of the merciful love of God.

Most likely, the weather is comfortable enough to enjoy the outdoors. Gather around the family table and talk about this project idea. Listen to everyone's suggestions for the perfect spot, and plan it out on paper. This dedicated outdoor prayer space might include a good-sized statue of Jesus or Mary (or both!). You might place stepping stones in the area, possibly a bench or chairs. You can plant pretty plants or flowers that will decorate your sacred space. Maybe you'll include a birdbath or statues of angels. Whatever you decide, no doubt you'll have fun creating it as a family and visiting it often for a family Rosary or other prayers.

NOTE TO PARENTS AND GRANDPARENTS

Talk to the children about the need to get rest and also be refreshed on Sunday—the Lord's Day but also to use their time wisely and not fill their minds with senseless or distracting media. Could you unplug from technology for a period of time (or all day!) today? As well, since this is "Harvested Sunday," ponder ways that you can "harvest" a teaching from your spiritual life and pass it on to others. Ask the family to ponder this as well. Put it into action soon.

MINI TEACHING

In the introduction, I mentioned the need to listen to God and reclaim our Sundays. I wrote, "God has set aside a full day each week for us to worship, rest, be refreshed, serve, and grow in holiness. At times, we have totally missed God's invitation because we either forgot, we weren't listening, or we were just too busy. We also need the reminders to slow down since life is packed with events. The Third Commandment is the reminder, 'Remember the Sabbath day, to keep it holy.'"

I also mentioned that the Catholic Catechism tells us, "The institution of Sunday helps all 'to be allowed sufficient rest and leisure to cultivate their familial, cultural, social, and religious lives'" (CCC, no. 2194). It couldn't be clearer: our Church wants us to slow down on Sundays— God wants us to.

In today's verse, Saint John Paul II points out the importance of not allowing our rest to "degenerate into emptiness or boredom." He teaches us that we must seek spiritual enrichment. Each day of our lives is yet another opportunity to grow in our Faith. We need to be mindful of what we read, watch, and listen to. We shouldn't put "garbage" (as my dear friend Father Bill used to say) into our heads. It will only bring us down, as well as haunt us at the most inopportune times. It is our responsibility as practicing Catholics to nourish our hearts and souls with solid Church teachings, not erroneous or watered-down material, and not ungodly stuff.

Take steps toward ensuring that your family is learning the Catholic Faith and seeking spiritual nourishment on a regular basis. Help them to do so and to "harvest" benefits from the teachings of holy Mother Church.

PONDER

Consider ways in which you can become more alive in your Faith. Think about ways you might spend more time in quiet meditation over a truth of the Faith. Make room for playing and laughing. Sundays are perfect days for love and laughter, after all.

FAMILY EVENING PRAYER
to be prayed each evening this week

Dear Lord, thank you for the blessings of this day—your day. If we have failed you in any way, please forgive us. If we have failed one another by not taking care of our responsibilities, please forgive us, Lord. Please help us to grow in holiness each day. We love you! Amen.

Pray: *Our Father, Hail Mary, Glory Be.*

Winter Sundays

"So that you may lead lives worthy of the Lord, fully pleasing to him, as you bear fruit in every good work and as you grow in the knowledge of God."
—Colossians 1:10

Wintertime can get so darn cold that I begin to dream about hibernating! I am not fond of cold weather, and therefore I tend to stay in the house as much as I can during the deep months of winter. Nestled in my home, I like to make big pots of nourishing and hearty soups, and I do a bit of healthy baking too. That is, in between visits with my children and grandchildren, writing my books, and traveling to speaking engagements. However, I do try to arrange my calendar so that I travel much less during winter months, trying to stay clear of icy streets and runways.

Cold, bleak days prod me to think of and pray for the less fortunate who might be shivering somewhere out in the cold, with nowhere to rest their heads. When I come upon these special souls, I like to offer them warm clothing: scarves, hats, or gloves, as well as a hot cup of nourishing soup and a promise of prayer. I usually give them a blessed Miraculous Medal as well. I feel that it's the very least I can do. Even if the winter season is not cold in your area, you can still do works of mercy that can help to warm someone's heart. Brainstorm together during this season and move out of your comfort zones to bring Christ's love to others!

CHAPTER 13

Board Games Sunday

"Bear with one another and, if anyone has a complaint against another, forgive each other; just as the Lord has forgiven you, so you also must forgive. Above all, clothe yourselves with love, which binds everything together in perfect harmony. And let the peace of Christ rule in your hearts, to which indeed you were called in the one body. And be thankful."

—Colossians 3:13–15

FAMILY MORNING PRAYER

Read the verse above and pray the Morning Offering together as a family.

Morning Offering: Dear Lord Jesus, thank you for the gift of today—your Sunday. Please guide our family as we strive to grow closer to you and to one another. Open our hearts and teach us to be much more generous with our time. Open our eyes to discover opportunities to love others. Amen.

Pray: *Our Father, Hail Mary, Glory Be.*

REFLECT

"Forgiveness" might be a tough pill to swallow, but it is an absolutely essential part of our spiritual lives. It might be difficult to forgive if we feel wounded by someone's ill actions toward us. As well, at times it's hard to ask for someone's forgiveness. Our pride might be standing in the way. However, we can certainly pray and ask God to grant graces to us so that we are able to forgive others and to ask for forgiveness.

Read again today's verse. How does it speak to your heart? Can you endeavor to impress the importance of this teaching to your family?

You'll want to talk to them about the need for forgiveness and to be clothed with Christ's love (through prayer and the sacraments). To drive the point home a bit further, have the children pray the Our Father prayer together. Ask them to slow down at the part, "Forgive us our trespasses as we forgive those who trespass against us." After finishing the prayer together, ask them to explain what it means. Encourage them to think about this question: *Should God forgive you the same way that you forgive others? Why or why not?* We need to be much more loving and forgiving.

CHOOSE AN ACTIVITY

Board games: Since this is "Board Games Sunday" it's time to get those board games out of the closet! Have the children choose three to five of their favorite board games. Now, to play board games properly, cell phones or other electronic devices are not allowed. Put them away. We should pay attention to one another while having a fun family time and not checking the latest status update or investigating the internet.

Though technology is not allowed during the playing of board games, conversation is indeed allowed! Now is the time to be lighthearted and even to plan a few goals while sitting together enjoying friendly board game competition. It's also a time to strive to keep "everything together in perfect harmony," as we read in today's verse. Hopefully, competitive arguments will not erupt during this time together. If so, firmly remind the family of that same verse. Read it aloud, if need be.

NOTE TO PARENTS AND GRANDPARENTS

Talk to the children about the need to get rest and be refreshed on the Lord's Day—about forgiveness and loving and praying for one another. Try to carry this theme throughout the day and the upcoming week. As well, if you do not do so already, use holy water more "religiously" (pun intended!). You will read about this below. You can get holy water from your parish church (for free!). My husband and I bring our empty holy water containers to the holy water supply on a regular basis!

MINI TEACHING

Be blessed: While you're at it, you might consider adding a decorative holy water font by the front door. Seeing the font there can be a reminder to bless yourself before you leave the house. Holy water is a powerful sacramental from our Church. The Church teaches, "Sacramentals derive from the baptismal priesthood: every baptized person is called to be a 'blessing,' and to bless" (CCC, no. 1669).

Holy water reminds us of our Baptism and our baptismal promises. The Church teaches, "Holy water is water that has been blessed by a priest and is used for various religious purposes such as blessings, dedications, exorcisms and the Asperges at the beginning of Mass. Holy Water is commonly found in a receptacle called a stoup or a font at the entrance of the church or in private homes so that the faithful may bless themselves with it" (CCC, no. 1170).

Holy water is a powerful tool in the spiritual life. I use holy water often in my home. My husband and I bless one another's forehead with holy water on our thumbs, making the Sign of the Cross. And we sprinkle it all around the house as well (especially around our bed at night before going to sleep).

Interestingly, the prayer said by the priest who blesses the holy water is quite elaborate and includes an exorcism. There are so many benefits to using holy water. The blessed water can drive away evil, protect us from illness and future illness, help us overcome temptation, and even help us to obtain actual graces (not sanctifying grace), which help us live out our life and vocation with holiness—being more open to God's Word.

We should use holy water often. Saint Thomas Aquinas and other Doctors of the Church have said the use of holy water can remove venial sin and temporal punishment. Saint Aquinas wrote, "By the sprinkling of Holy Water the debt of venial sin is wiped out; but not always, however, are all temporal punishments relinquished."[5] That would depend upon our contrition for sin and our love and faith in God.

Saint Teresa of Avila extolled the use of holy water. She said, "I have myself felt an extraordinary consolation when I have used holy water.

It is certain that I have felt a great joy and inner peace which I cannot describe, a joy with which my soul was quite refreshed. . . . It comforts me to see the great power which her [the Church's] blessing imparts to water, so great is the difference between blessed and unblessed water."[6] Saint Teresa also stated that holy water makes demons flee! She said it was the only means she knew that prevents them from coming back. So, I highly encourage you to use this holy sacramental—and to use it often! I decided a while back that when I give a house-warming gift to a Catholic family, I will include a large bottle of holy water and a holy water font for them to hang near their front door.

PONDER

Consider ways in which you can become more alive in your Faith. Could you use Church sacramentals more often? Make plenty of room for playing and laughing! I hope you will play board games! Make marvelous memories for your family.

FAMILY EVENING PRAYER

to be prayed each evening this week

Dear Lord, thank you for the blessings of this day—your day. If we have failed you in any way, please forgive us. If we have failed one another by not taking care of our responsibilities, please forgive us, Lord. Please help us to grow in holiness each day. We love you! Amen.

Pray: *Our Father, Hail Mary, Glory Be.*

CHAPTER 14

Mug-a-Soup Sunday

"On Sundays and other holy days of obligation, the faithful are obliged to assist at Mass. They are also to abstain from such work or business that would inhibit the worship to be given to God, the joy proper to the Lord's Day, or the due relaxation of mind and body."
—Code of Canon Law, no. 1247

FAMILY MORNING PRAYER

Read the verse above and pray the Morning Offering together as a family.

Morning Offering: Dear Lord Jesus, thank you for the gift of today—your Sunday. Please guide our family as we strive to grow closer to you and to one another. Open our hearts and teach us to be much more generous with our time. Open our eyes to discover opportunities to love others today and always. Amen.

Pray: *Our Father, Hail Mary, Glory Be.*

REFLECT

As we have been discussing throughout this book, Sunday, our Lord's Day, is supposed to be observed with worship (as today's verse above from Canon Law states), and with honoring our Lord by abstaining "from such work or business that would inhibit the worship to be given to God, the joy proper to the Lord's Day, or the due relaxation of mind and body."

Our Church also teaches that, in addition, we should do our best to ensure that others don't have to do unnecessary work on Sundays:

Sanctifying Sundays and holy days requires a common effort. Every Christian should avoid making unnecessary demands on others that would hinder them from observing the Lord's Day. Traditional activities (sport, restaurants, etc.), and social necessities (public services, etc.), require some people to work on Sundays, but everyone should still take care to set aside sufficient time for leisure. With temperance and charity the faithful will see to it that they avoid the excesses and violence sometimes associated with popular leisure activities. In spite of economic constraints, public authorities should ensure citizens a time intended for rest and divine worship. Employers have a similar obligation toward their employees.

(CCC, no. 2187)

Let's be sure that we don't keep ourselves so busy that we neglect to give God the proper worship due to him, time to help someone in need with works of mercy, and the relaxation of our minds and body, which is necessary for us.

CHOOSE AN ACTIVITY

Healthy soup: Consider making a large pot of healthy soup soon. Many times, I make two big pots of soup so that I'll have enough to share. Find recipes online or in a cookbook. Better yet—make a soup that is traditional to your family or heritage. Did your grandmother or aunt make a special soup? If you don't know, if possible, call them up and ask! Ask someone else in the family who might know. Don't put it off until another time. Time is a'tickin. If you can't find a family recipe, research a type of soup that is part of your heritage and enjoy making and eating it!

Seize the moment to share a family tradition with your young ones, as well as to spend time in the kitchen together cooking your soup. You can enjoy it at dinner, possibly along with healthy bread or muffins. Hopefully, you will decide to bring some hot soup to a relative, a neighbor, or someone from your parish who would welcome your meal made with love.

NOTE TO PARENTS AND GRANDPARENTS

Talk to the children about the need to plan to spend time together with the family, to worship God, to learn more about the Faith, and to get rest and refreshment on Sunday. The world outside your domestic church beckons for the children's attention. However, your warm encouragement to be involved with the family today, as well as your presence to them, speaks volumes and sets robust traditions of family togetherness.

MINI TEACHING

We will discuss Saint Faustina later, in another chapter, but for now I'd love to tell you a fascinating true story that fits right in with our "Mug-a-Soup Sunday." To do so, I'll share an excerpt from my book *52 Weeks with Saint Faustina: A Year of Grace and Mercy*:

An Extraordinary Visit

One gloomy day, the bell at the gate rang. Sister Faustina looked out through sheets of rain to see a shivering young man persistently ringing the bell. The rain poured down with a vengeance, soaking the man to the skin. As soon as Sr. Faustina answered the gate, the fellow asked for something to eat. Sister Faustina ran to the kitchen and couldn't find anything to offer. She was determined to help that young, unfortunate man. There had to be something in the kitchen. Finally, she found it—some wholesome soup; the perfect remedy to combat the icy rain while providing nourishment. She heated it up straightaway. Sister Faustina then added some pieces of bread on top to help fill his hungry belly and rushed the hot mug of soup to the poor beggar waiting in the rain. The stranger accepted the charitable meal from the sister's hands and consumed it right there by the gate. He seemed to enjoy it despite the inclement weather. Sister Faustina took the empty mug from the man's cold wet hands, and to her great surprise, discovered that the poor man was actually Jesus Christ Himself! He then immediately vanished from her sight. Sister Faustina later reflected upon the encounter. She heard an interior voice: "My daughter, the blessings of the poor who bless Me as they leave this gate have reached My ears. And your compassion, within the bounds of obedience, has pleased Me, and this is why I came down from My throne—to taste the fruits of your mercy" (*Diary*, 1312). Can we even imagine this?

Read the story to the children and tell them that God calls us to serve others with love. St. Faustina was truly serving Jesus in the beggar, and Jesus let her know!

In Matthew's Gospel, Jesus very clearly instructs that what we do and do not do to others we actually do to him. Specifically, he said, "Truly I tell you, just as you did it to one of the least of these who are members of my family, you did it to me" (Matt. 25:40). As well, Jesus also said, "Truly I tell you, just as you did not do it to one of the least of these, you did not do it to me" (Matt. 25:45). Impress upon the children that their actions and lack thereof always have consequences. God is always aware.

PONDER

Take time to consider ways in which you can become more alive in your Faith. Seek opportunities to live your Faith and teach it too. Don't forget to smile! Have fun with the family. Slow down to enjoy your family. When time allows, make some soup!

FAMILY EVENING PRAYER

to be prayed each evening this week

Dear Lord, thank you for the blessings of this day—your day. If we have failed you in any way, please forgive us. If we have failed one another by not taking care of our responsibilities, please forgive us, Lord. Please help us to grow in holiness each day. We love you! Amen.

Pray: *Our Father, Hail Mary, Glory Be.*

CHAPTER 15

Make a Snowman Sunday

"Honor your father and your mother, as the Lord your God commanded you, so that your days may be long and that it may go well with you in the land that the LORD your God is giving you."
—Deuteronomy 5:16

FAMILY MORNING PRAYER

Read the verse above and pray the Morning Offering together as a family.

Morning Offering: Dear Lord Jesus, thank you for the gift of today—your Sunday. Please guide our family as we strive to grow closer to you and to one another. Open our hearts and teach us to be much more generous with our time. Open our eyes to discover opportunities to love others. Amen.

Pray: *Our Father, Hail Mary, Glory Be.*

REFLECT

The winter season often has a negative effect on certain people's moods. There is something called Seasonal Affective Disorder (SAD). While SAD is still a bit of a mystery to experts, some say that the ions in the air, heredity, and brain chemicals might be involved. Whatever the case, the cold temperatures, the dreary gray winter days, and in many places, the shorter days and lack of enough sunlight can cause folks to feel depressed or a bit blue.

If not suffering from SAD, some people experience "cabin fever," or a feeling of being "stuck" inside for too long—perhaps due to cold temperatures or inclement weather, as well as a disability that keeps them homebound. They might feel a bit trapped. Because of these afflictions that surface in the wintertime, it's a good idea to be mindful of people who suffer with such maladies and to do what we can to reach out to them during winter months. Consider making homemade nutritious soup or a hot meal to take to your elderly neighbors. Have the children create cheery, colorful greeting cards that you can give to them as well. Your loving gestures and care will no doubt bring light into their lives, and your children will learn a valuable lesson.

Pray and ponder loving works of mercy that your family can do for others during the dreary months of winter. Even a simple phone call and a special time chatting with someone who feels lonely will surely help them with their battle with the winter blues. Encouraging and loving words do go a very long way!

CHOOSE AN ACTIVITY

Make a snowman: Since it's wintertime and today is "Make a Snowman Sunday," make a snowman together! That's if there's any snow outside. Could you get together around the kitchen table and create winter artwork? Perhaps draw a family of "snow people"? Talk to your children about the importance of family and about honoring your father and mother while doing your craft. You might role play with the family of snowmen. How about enjoying a cup of hot chocolate with marshmallows while each family member takes a turn at telling a creative (made up on the spot!) story?

You also might want to try out a new recipe that you look up together or one you've learned from a relative. You can catch up with an older relative by phone and ask about their favorite recipe while you're at it!

Works of mercy: Start planning a few works of mercy for anyone you know who might feel alone, depressed, or who is experiencing the winter blues. How about gifting them with handmade smiling snowman greeting cards? Reaching out to assist the less fortunate is extremely worthwhile and pleasing to God.

NOTE TO PARENTS AND GRANDPARENTS

The world is a busy place. But Sunday in your domestic church can have a marvelous sense of peace and security. It should be an oasis for the family. Talk to the children about how cutting down on technology use can help us to be more attentive to life as it unfolds around us as well as rests our weary brains. With your continual encouragement and example, in time, your children will come to expect that Sundays are indeed set apart from the other days of the week.

MINI TEACHING

Today, we also want to place importance on the Fourth Commandment of honoring our father and mother, especially in a time when it seems that our world has lost much respect for life in the family. Talk to the children about the Fourth Commandment. Read today's verse (Deut. 5:16). The Catechism teaches: "The fourth commandment opens the second table of the Decalogue. It shows us the order of charity. God has willed that, after him, we should honor our parents to whom we owe life and who have handed on to us the knowledge of God. We are obliged to honor and respect all those whom God, for our good, has vested with his authority" (CCC, no. 2197).

Take some time today to emphasize this important teaching. Could you also say a few extra prayers today for unfortunate families who are fragmented and do not experience the love of God within their own wounded family?

PONDER

Consider ways you can become more alive in your Faith. As you pray, ask God to continue to guide you in guiding your family on the straight and narrow path that leads to heaven. Always make room for worshiping, resting, playing and laughing! You will set an invaluable lesson in observing the Lord's Day.

FAMILY EVENING PRAYER
to be prayed each evening this week

Dear Lord, thank you for the blessings of this day—your day. If we have failed you in any way, please forgive us. If we have failed one another by not taking care of our responsibilities, please forgive us, Lord. Please help us to grow in holiness each day. We love you! Amen.

Pray: *Our Father, Hail Mary, Glory Be.*

Warming Our Neighbor Sunday

"How does God's love abide in anyone who has the world's goods and sees a brother or sister in need and yet refuses help?"
—1 John 3:17

FAMILY MORNING PRAYER

Read the verse above and pray the Morning Offering together as a family.

Morning Offering: Dear Lord Jesus, thank you for the gift of today—your Sunday. Please guide our family as we strive to grow closer to you and to one another. Open our hearts and teach us to be much more generous with our time. Open our eyes to discover opportunities to love others. Amen.

Pray: *Our Father, Hail Mary, Glory Be.*

REFLECT

Because it is wintertime, our thoughts might often be on the needy—the people who might be homeless or those who lack the necessities of life—which might include warm clothing or food.

Today's chapter is "Warming Our Neighbor Sunday." Today's verse talks about refusing to help someone in need. More precisely, it puts forth the question about how one with God's love and the means to help can possibly refuse to do so. This is certainly something that faithful Catholics should ponder often.

How are we helping or not helping those in need? Of course, we are not expected to physically help every soul on this planet. That is why there are so many of us—to help one another! We can certainly pray for each one. We know that we are to love God, but we are also called to love our neighbor. As well, we are not simply to love them, but to love them as ourselves! The Bible tells us, "The second is this, 'You shall love your neighbor as yourself.' There is no other commandment greater than these" (Mk. 12:31). Try your best to carry this theme throughout today and this week to impress it upon your family.

CHOOSE AN ACTIVITY

A holy field trip: If desired, take time to research local places of pilgrimage. It might be a cathedral, the home site of a saint, a convent, a basilica, or a monastery. Get the family involved, asking their opinions about where they'd like to go someday. Assign "homework" to family members who are able to do some research on a holy destination. Ask them to report back to the dinner table in the upcoming week with three interesting facts about it.

I have visited a monastery in which an entire room was dedicated to first-class relics of numerous saints! This would certainly be a big plus to an upcoming visit. You can research online or in books or articles about the saints to become more familiar with them before venerating their relics together as a family. Prior to your holy field trip, you might decide to pray a nine-day novena to one of the saints, asking for their intercession for your family.

Warming your neighbor: Brainstorm together to discern ways that your family could help "a brother or sister in need" as today's verse states. Since we are in the winter season, what ways can you keep your "neighbor" warm? I have often gifted the unfortunate that I come upon with warm hand-knitted scarves, as well as cups of hot soup, and other items. On the underside of each scarf I have sewn blessed religious medals. I point them out to the recipients and also promise my prayers. Try to move beyond what's comfortable to carry out meaningful works of mercy with your family.

NOTE TO PARENTS AND GRANDPARENTS

Talk to the children about the need to get along with one another in the family, perhaps more especially on Sundays. Let them know that God has specifically chosen them to live, love, grow, and learn together. Encourage them to take a break from too much technology and get rest to be refreshed on Sunday—the Lord's Day.

MINI TEACHING

"Extra credit" spiritual exercise for the adults and older children!

Saint Margaret Mary Alacoque reminds us to work hard at getting to heaven. She said, "Let us begin in earnest to work out our salvation, for no one will do it for us, since even He Himself, Who made us without ourselves, will not save us without ourselves."[7] It's essential for each of us to place importance on getting our hearts and souls in order. As a parent, grandparent, or caregiver, we have to be in good shape in order to help those under our care. Ponder ways that you can work out your salvation in the midst of your daily life. You might ask yourself a few questions:

> Do I try to see challenges as opportunities for prayer and grace?
> Do I try to carve out extra prayer time whenever I can? Or, do I clutter my time with senseless activity (too much internet, television, or social media)?
> Do I strive to be an exemplary example of holiness?
> What changes can I make in my schedule to be more available to listen to God's whispers to my soul?

Building our domestic church to nourish our family's hearts and souls is certainly part of working out our own salvation that we read about in St. Margaret Mary Alacoque's words above. Our sincere and loving efforts will indeed help others as well.

PONDER

Consider ways you can become more alive in your Faith. Have fun with the family. In addition to good works and worship, carve out time for rest too. You will be setting a wonderful example of properly observing Sunday.

FAMILY EVENING PRAYER

to be prayed each evening this week

Dear Lord, thank you for the blessings of this day—your day. If we have failed you in any way, please forgive us. If we have failed one another by not taking care of our responsibilities, please forgive us, Lord. Please help us to grow in holiness each day. We love you! Amen.

Pray: *Our Father, Hail Mary, Glory Be.*

PART FIVE

Lenten Sundays

"Yet even now, says the LORD, return to me with all your heart, with fasting, with weeping, and with mourning; rend your hearts and not your clothing. Return to the LORD, your God, for he is gracious and merciful, slow to anger, and abounding in steadfast love, and relents from punishing."
—Joel 2:12–13

Holy Mother Church gifts us with the penitential season of Lent. It is a perfect time to press the "pause button," and try to slow down a bit so that we can pray more attentively. Lent is a distinctive and holy season of forty days on our Church's calendar. The number forty is significant. There are many times throughout salvation history when the number forty was important. But for now, we focus on the fact that Jesus fasted for forty days in the wilderness. During Lent, we are called to fast, give alms, and pray so the bonds that are holding us back spiritually can be broken and we can grow closer to God.

The season of Lent is meant to transform hearts and souls. In order for true transformation to happen, though, we need to wholeheartedly apply ourselves so that we are not just simply giving up chocolate or another pleasure for a period of time. We should really want to rise to the challenge. These forty days, we can truly make extra efforts and grow in the spiritual life.

CHAPTER 17

Unplug Sunday

"Just as God 'rested on the seventh day from all his work which he had done,' human life has a rhythm of work and rest. The institution of the Lord's Day helps everyone enjoy adequate rest and leisure to cultivate their familial, cultural, social, and religious lives."

—Catechism of the Catholic Church, no. 2184

FAMILY MORNING PRAYER

Read the verse above and pray the Morning Offering together as a family.

Morning Offering: Dear Lord Jesus, thank you for the gift of today—your Sunday. Please guide our family as we strive to grow closer to you and to one another. Open our hearts and teach us to be much more generous with our time. Open our eyes to discover opportunities to love others. Amen.

Pray: *Our Father, Hail Mary, Glory Be.*

REFLECT

Don't run away: Perhaps the title of this chapter is a bit scary in an age of technology. However, I have confidence in you to rise to the occasion! Remember, Saint John Paul II said, "Be not afraid!" Truly, *every* Sunday should be "Unplug Sunday." At least for today, try your best to unplug from unnecessary media. Enjoy peace and quiet in which to immerse your body, heart, mind, and soul.

In today's verse, we learn, "human life has a rhythm of work and rest." How does that speak to your heart? Have you noticed a rhythm? If not, why is that? Could you strive to take steps to have more of a balance in your life? Can you be mindful not to "burn the candle at both ends" and wear yourself out? One way to achieve a more peaceful heart and mind is to step away from too much technology use, as well as to carve out more time to speak with your Creator. Did you notice that I said, "with" and not "to"? That is because the conversation with God has to be two-sided. We must make room for God and work at silencing our minds (and lips) enough to hear God speak to our hearts. Ponder this.

CHOOSE AN ACTIVITY

Unplug and refresh: Remember that young lady in the news a while back who fell into a fountain because she was walking while texting on her cell phone? It might seem a bit funny, but it's actually not! How often we feel a need to check our devices for the newest status update or something or another. It's become a bad habit in most cases. Sure, I will admit that I am an avid user of technology, and the media too. After all, at least three of our popes (St. John Paul II, Benedict XVI, and Pope Francis) have encouraged us to use the media for good to counteract the evil that moves through. it. As well, I enjoy the use of technology to stay in touch with my family.

I have to be extra careful with my use of technology. We all do, really. If I'm not mindful and sensible about my need for rest, my "office light" might not get turned off at the end of the day because of that thing called a "smartphone" that we carry in our back pockets or purses (aka my little "office") and that is ever-beckoning. So, while I attempt to use technology only for good, to stay in touch with family, for work, and to evangelize, I am also extremely mindful of my use of technology. I don't want to allow it take over my life and cause me to miss rest, as well as miss many opportunities to converse with others, share my heart, and listen with attention to those who need to be heard.

I dare you: See if you can "unplug" completely from unnecessary technology today. By doing so, you will free your mind and attention to focus on life as it unfolds around you. It can be so refreshing to experience real life without countless added technology distractions. As well, using technology too often can cause a person to feel that they are always "on call," so to speak. Their minds don't get a chance to rest properly. Our challenging era necessitates that we fight the urge to be ever available for the bombardment of technology through media, advertising, and more.

Let's talk: Now that you will "unplug" today, you will certainly be gloriously unhampered to enjoy wonderful family conversations and experiences together, untethered as you will be from technology! Enjoy the freedom! I hope it becomes a Sunday habit!

NOTE TO PARENTS AND GRANDPARENTS

Impress upon the children the importance of establishing a proper balance in their lives. Remind them that Sunday is a special day to enjoy the family, to worship God at Mass, to nourish one's faith by praying and spiritual reading, as well as to reach out in mercy to help others in need. Your encouragement will be an integral part of their faith formation and foundation!

MINI TEACHING

In the opening chapters of Genesis, we see a pattern of work and rest is established—God worked and he rested. Certainly, God, with his infinite power, did not need to rest after creating heaven and earth. However, he chose to rest, and it seems that he found rest to be refreshing. He set the example for his children. In today's verse, we learn about the "rhythm of work and rest." Because this balance is essential to a healthy spiritual life, many religious orders have this rhythm built into their rules and statutes. They pray, work, and rest to stay balanced and healthy.

We might consider the fact that Jesus went off to the wilderness to fast and pray for forty days and nights. He retreated from the world of distraction to listen to his Father, to pray deeply, and to prepare for his work. Mother Teresa often turned to silence to listen to God's whispers. She took herself away from her often backbreaking work by wisely retreating to the chapel for certain scheduled times of prayer in which to nourish her heart and soul while in the presence of Jesus in the Blessed

Sacrament. She made sure that each Sister did the same. Though for the most part strenuous, their days were very structured to have a proper balance. Our Lord's words, "Be still and know that I am God," call to our hearts. Do your best to endeavor to be still—on a regular basis—to listen to our Lord and allow him to recharge your batteries.

PONDER

Consider fasting from unnecessary technology every Sunday if you can. Encourage the kids to do so as well. One important step to making that happen is in not giving in to their pleading to have a smartphone like their friends. I often write about and speak about this topic, and I think I could actually write an entire book on the importance of keeping the young ones away from the internet and cell phones for as long as possible. Have fun with your family. Make room for playing and laughing! Get your rest and refreshment. Enjoy every bit. All the while, you are creating warm experiences and memories for your family. Smile! Smile again. It's contagious!

FAMILY EVENING PRAYER

to be prayed each evening this week

Dear Lord, thank you for the blessings of this day—your day. If we have failed you in any way, please forgive us. If we have failed one another by not taking care of our responsibilities, please forgive us, Lord. Please help us to grow in holiness each day. We love you! Amen.

Pray: *Our Father, Hail Mary, Glory Be.*

CHAPTER 18

Be Attentive Sunday

"Above all, maintain constant love for one another, for love covers a multitude of sins. Be hospitable to one another without complaining. Like good stewards of the manifold grace of God, serve one another with whatever gift each of you has received."
—1 Peter 4:8–10

FAMILY MORNING PRAYER

Read the verse above and pray the Morning Offering together as a family.

Morning Offering: Dear Lord Jesus, thank you for the gift of today—your Sunday. Please guide our family as we strive to grow closer to you and to one another. Open our hearts and teach us to be much more generous with our time. Open our eyes to discover opportunities to love others. Amen.

Pray: *Our Father, Hail Mary, Glory Be.*

REFLECT

Talk to the family about the need to be more attentive to the needs of others. Read aloud today's verse again. Ask the children to be good to one another—to be loving—without complaining. Next, ask them to think about their God-given gifts. Are they aware of them? Sometimes the best way for them to discover their own gifts is when others point them out. Ask them if they are a good listener; a kind person; a good pray-er; a good artist; a good problem solver; a good storyteller; a good comforter; a good student; a good child of God; a good sports person. And the list goes on. Help them to realize their God-given gifts. This exercise will benefit the entire family. Ask the children to list three ways in which they can help others with the gifts that they possess. Encourage them to write them down and to put them into action.

CHOOSE AN ACTIVITY

Learn about saints for the Lenten Season: Choose one or more saints from the list below and do your own research about the saint. Share your information with the family at the dinner table. Encourage the children to draw a picture after hearing you share about the saint. In hearing their story or stories, you might be inspired to do a craft or make a meal that relates to particular saints. Have fun learning! Remember, you are establishing an invaluable spiritual foundation for your family.

March 3: Saint Katharine Drexel

March 4: Saint Casimir

March 7: Saints Perpetua and Felicity

March 8: Saint John of God

March 9: Saint Frances of Rome

March 17: Saint Patrick

March 18: Saint Cyril of Jerusalem

March 19: Solemnity of Saint Joseph, Husband of the Blessed Virgin Mary

March 23: Saint Toribio of Mogrovejo

March 25: Solemnity of the Annunciation of the Lord

April 4: Saint Isidore

April 5: Saint Vincent Ferrer

April 7: Saint John Baptist de la Salle

Extra credit: After learning about the saint or saints, ask the children what special gifts they possessed: Ask them if they can try to emulate the virtues of the saints you learned about and saints in general, reminding the family that saints were just normal people like they are, but they chose to try hard in the spiritual life to please God and help others to get to heaven. They practiced heroic virtues. Let them know that they can do it too—day by day.

NOTE TO PARENTS AND GRANDPARENTS

Talk to the children about the need to spend time together as a family, especially on Sundays, to worship God at Mass, to get along with others, and to help others in need by serving them with their gifts. As well, I continue to remind you, it is important to get rest and also be refreshed on Sunday. I need reminders too!

MINI TEACHING

The season of Lent is meant to transform our hearts and souls. As I mentioned at the start of this part of the book, "In order for true transformation to happen, though, we need to wholeheartedly apply ourselves so that we are not just simply giving up chocolate or some other pleasure for a period of time." Can we rise to the challenge? During these forty days, when we truly make some extra efforts, we will certainly grow in the spiritual life. The Lenten season invites us to walk with Jesus, to relive the forty days that he prayed and fasted in the wilderness before he began his public ministry—which as we know, culminated in the sacrifice of the Cross—which, as St. John Paul II said, was "the definitive victory over death."

I love what St. John Paul II expressed about Lent. He said, "The time of Lent is a special time for purification and penance as to allow our Savior to make us His neighbor and save us by His love. . . . The liturgical period of Lent is given us in and through the Church in order to purify us of that remainder of selfishness and excessive attachment to things, material or otherwise, which keep us apart from those who have a right to our help: principally those who, whether physically near or far, are unable to live their lives with dignity as men and women created by God in his image and likeness."[8] I'm reminded of Jesus's instructions in Matthew 25:45, "Whatever you did to the least of who are members of my family, you did to me." Let's keep those words in mind throughout this Lenten season and beyond. Ask the family how they can walk with Jesus during this Lenten season and how they have been walking with him thus far. Share these thoughts soon at the dinner table. Ask them (with your help) to write down their thoughts and resolutions and post them so they will be reminded.

PONDER

Take time to ponder ways in which you can become more alive in your Faith. As you pray, allow God to heal you and make you new, so you will be an exemplary Christian example to your family and others. Enjoy your Sunday together. Live in every moment. Thank God for your family! Tell him out loud.

FAMILY EVENING PRAYER
to be prayed each evening this week

Dear Lord, thank you for the blessings of this day—your day. If we have failed you in any way, please forgive us. If we have failed one another by not taking care of our responsibilities, please forgive us, Lord. Please help us to grow in holiness each day. We love you! Amen.

Pray: *Our Father, Hail Mary, Glory Be.*

CHAPTER 19

Show Your Love Sunday

"I give you a new commandment, that you love one another. Just as I have loved you, you also should love one another. By this everyone will know that you are my disciples, if you have love for one another."

—John 13:34–35

FAMILY MORNING PRAYER

Read the verse above and pray the Morning Offering together as a family.

Morning Offering: Dear Lord Jesus, thank you for the gift of today—your Sunday. Please guide our family as we strive to grow closer to you and to one another. Open our hearts and teach us to be much more generous with our time. Open our eyes to discover opportunities to love others. Amen.

Pray: *Our Father, Hail Mary, Glory Be.*

REFLECT

Get into the habit of offering your day to the Lord first thing every morning. As soon as you open your eyes, tell him you love him. Thank him for the new day. Offer all your prayers, hopes, joys, and sufferings in the words of the formal Morning Offering or in your own words. Ask God to take care of everything. Each Sunday throughout *Reclaiming Sundays* you have been encouraged to pray a simple Morning Offering with your family.

After getting your day off to the right start, endeavor to lift your heart to Jesus all throughout the day. Encourage the children to do the same. You can help them form healthy prayer habits of striking up conversations with God. By being in a habit of taking the time in the morning for prayer with your Savior and then again throughout the day, you'll be keeping up a "heart-to-heart" with Jesus. You'll be praying "always" as we are instructed in Scripture. In addition, your family prayers together in using *Reclaiming Sundays* will be a practice your children will long remember. We can certainly hope and pray that within their own future domestic churches they will carry on these prayer habits and practices that you teach now.

CHOOSE AN ACTIVITY

Lenten love notes: Spend time together at the kitchen or dining room table to create sweet love notes that you will anonymously gift to others. When gathered together, read today's verse aloud. Ask the children to comment on its meaning.

Gather the materials that you will find listed below.

Together, look up inspiring verses from the Bible.

Fold craft or art paper in half to create several greeting cards.

Have the children draw on them, add stickers, and decorate colorfully to their hearts content!

Add the inspiring Scripture verses and/or an original short note, such as: We hope you are smiling today! We hope this card will bring a smile to your face! We hope you are doing well! We are thinking of you—we love you! Remember to say a prayer today. God loves you! And so on. The idea is to surprise people with anonymous love notes. Your beautiful handmade cards and prayers to go along with them can certainly help to lift spirits.

Pray an Our Father, Hail Mary, and a Glory Be for all the people who will receive your "Lenten love notes."

Put the notes in the mail without a return address and without signing them. However, if the children would like to send cards to relatives, neighbors, or friends, by all means, do that as well. In addition, some cards may not require postage stamps if you don't need to send them through the mail.

If you choose to create "Lenten love notes" you will need:

This book (to read the verse above)

The Bible

Pencils, crayons, markers, paints, paper, stickers, and any other craft supplies that you would like to use to make cards

Postage stamps

Envelopes

Have fun and be creative!

NOTE TO PARENTS AND GRANDPARENTS

Talk to the children about family togetherness on Sundays. Let them know that you value their presence in your home, that you delight in their contributions and conversations, and that they should strive to be home on Sundays whenever possible. Today we focus on loving others as we journey through Lent. Do your best to carry out the theme through-out the upcoming week. When time allows, check the back of the book for tips on "Building Your Domestic Church."

MINI TEACHING

Lent is an opportunity to experience a true conversion of heart. Some people think that a conversion only happens once in a lifetime. True conversion is ongoing. During the season of Lent, holy Mother Church encourages the faithful to slow down and to pay attention. Rather than focus upon our own needs, Lent is a time to grow closer to God and to pray that we can help others with their needs. God's love inspires us to do so. Through prayer, we are to become more Christlike. We are to become more like his loving Mother Mary.

Lent consists of these three pillars: prayer, fasting, and almsgiving. By fasting and giving up things as a form of penance, by praying, and by giving alms, we can learn self-control and Christian charity, and we will grow in holiness. Our almsgiving can be in the form of a contribution to a charity, but also in the form of a charitable word or deed. During this holy season we should carve out additional times to be with God—to listen to him and share with him. He will fill our hearts with great graces if we will slow down, pay attention, and surrender our hearts fully to him. Allow this Lenten journey to be transformative in your own heart and ultimately in the hearts of those around you.

PONDER

Consider ways you can become more alive in your Faith, especially during such a holy season. Slow down and converse with God. Have fun with the family, creating educational and fun experiences, as well as warm memories.

FAMILY EVENING PRAYER

to be prayed each evening this week

Dear Lord, thank you for the blessings of this day—your day. If we have failed you in any way, please forgive us. If we have failed one another by not taking care of our responsibilities, please forgive us, Lord. Please help us to grow in holiness each day. We love you! Amen.

Pray: *Our Father, Hail Mary, Glory Be.*

CHAPTER 20

Feeding the Hungry Sunday

"Let us remember well however, that whenever food is thrown out it is as if it were stolen from the table of the poor, from the hungry! I ask everyone to reflect on the problem of the loss and waste of food, to identify ways and approaches which, by seriously dealing with this problem, convey solidarity and sharing with the underprivileged."
—Pope Francis, General Audience, June 5, 2013

FAMILY MORNING PRAYER

Read the verse above and pray the Morning Offering together as a family.

Morning Offering: Dear Lord Jesus, thank you for the gift of today—your Sunday. Please guide our family as we strive to grow closer to you and to one another. Open our hearts and teach us to be much more generous with our time. Open our eyes to discover opportunities to love others. Amen.

Pray: *Our Father, Hail Mary, Glory Be.*

REFLECT

Pope Francis's words in today's verse speak about not wasting, as well as our unambiguous responsibility to care for the poor. Pope Francis certainly reminds me of Mother Teresa, whom I was very blessed to know personally. Both Mother Teresa and Pope Francis were very concerned about the poor and hungry. While navigating this sacrificial season of Lent, what can your family do to help lessen the hunger pains of the hungry and unfortunate? Could you possibly fast this week and use the food you would have eaten to make something nutritious for the unfortunate in your community?

Mother Teresa was famous for saying, "Love begins at home." Look into the needs in your local community. Where is help needed the most? Is there a local soup kitchen? Is there a family that could use help? Discuss ways in which you can help others this Lenten season and beyond, as well as the importance of not wasting food. Ask the children to list three ways that they can be helpful with this. Write them down, and do your best to carry them out.

CHOOSE AN ACTIVITY

Lenten meals: Do your best to plan at least a couple of meals that you can make together during this Lenten season that you will gift to needy families. Ask your parish or local soup kitchen where help is needed the most. Perhaps you can make a recipe that was a favorite for a particular saint. Make a double recipe so you can gift it to someone in need. Again, do a bit of research when time allows, and check the back of this book if you need ideas for activities.

Family Adoration: Find time during this Lenten season to visit our Lord in the Blessed Sacrament at your parish church or an Adoration chapel. Try to do this as often as possible. Prepare the children by telling them that Jesus is truly there—Body, Blood, Soul, and Divinity. He welcomes your visits. With little ones (because they might get restless), it's best not to expect too much time at Adoration. Any amount of time is a plus! Consider praying a family Rosary (or decade) together. As well, pray for all those who have asked your prayers and for the poor, hungry, and anyone who is struggling.

NOTE TO PARENTS AND GRANDPARENTS

Talk to the children about not wasting their food and the need to help others who are less fortunate. Remind them that the Lenten season beckons us to listen more attentively to God and to make more time for him throughout our days. He needs to be right at the top of their "to-do" lists!

Endeavor to carve out a period of time today (even 15 or 20 minutes) for them to close their eyes and talk to God in their own words.

MINI TEACHING

Some of us might remember our parents telling us to eat up all our food at the dinner table because there were starving children on the other side of the world. Most likely, we didn't understand, and we might joke about it now as adults suggesting that our parents were going to scoop up our leftover peas and carrots and ship them off to China or somewhere!

I'll never forget sitting in a New York City McDonald's restaurant with Servant of God Father John Hardon, sj (my friend and spiritual director whose canonization cause has opened), and my family. I can picture it vividly. Father Hardon never ate out at fancy restaurants, taking seriously his vow of poverty. If you were going to dine with him, it would have to be at a retreat, a convent, a monastery, or a fast-food restaurant.

Jessica, my youngest at the time, was just a toddler and had left a few French fries on her tray. She couldn't eat anything more. She was also a bit restless and wanted to get out of that little fast-food establishment to stretch her legs to embark upon a new adventure. As Jessica wriggled in her seat, Father Hardon glanced down at the abandoned stray French fries. With penetrating eyes, he looked up into mine.

"What would Mother Teresa say?" Those were his succinct words. I found myself at a loss for words in that moment. Knowing Mother Teresa for about a decade and spending time in one of her New York City convents and soup kitchens further impacted my desire to not waste any food. I will occasionally get into conversations with the wait staff at restaurants explaining why I am taking home the remainder of the meal that I couldn't finish, as well as the leftover bread (that they will throw away and that I know that someone hungry will appreciate).

In a General Audience (and today's verse), Pope Francis stated, "Let us remember well however, that whenever food is thrown out it is as if it were stolen from the table of the poor, from the hungry!" Ask the children to be more cognizant about not wasting food.

PONDER

Ponder ways in which you can become more alive in your Faith. Allow God to make you new so you will be an exemplary Christian example to your family and others. Have fun with the family. They will look back on these family times in years to come, happy for the family Sundays!

FAMILY EVENING PRAYER
to be prayed each evening this week

Dear Lord, thank you for the blessings of this day—your day. If we have failed you in any way, please forgive us. If we have failed one another by not taking care of our responsibilities, please forgive us, Lord. Please help us to be mindful of wasting food and to do all we can to feed the poor. Help us to grow in holiness each day. We love you! Amen.

Pray: *Our Father, Hail Mary, Glory Be.*

Easter Season Sundays

"Do not abandon yourselves to despair. We are the Easter people and hallelujah is our song."
—Saint John Paul II[9]

S aint John Paul II's words prod us to keep our eyes fixed on heaven and its rewards. Similar words were spoken by St. Augustine back in the fourth century. Both these saints experienced feeling on the brink of despair because of turbulent landscapes in their motherlands. St. John Paul II added the first line to Augustine's triumphant statement. He reminded us of what *not* to do. "Do not abandon yourselves to despair." Because the world might seem to be "going to hell in a hand basket," some might feel tempted to abandon themselves to despair. But God does not want that at all! Despair is a sin and the devil uses it for his gain. Giving in to despair means we don't trust our Lord to bring us up and out of this messy life. Of course, there are those who aren't able to help themselves from falling into despair, and our Lord won't fault them for that.

We are here to help them. They are our brothers and sisters. We start first within our families and then broaden our reach. Certainly, God places specific people in our lives. Let's be attentive to their needs and show them Christ's love to lift them up from any darkness or fear. We can also try to point them in the direction of therapy, if need be. Throughout this Easter season (which consists of fifty days and seven Sundays), keep your eyes lifted toward heaven and its rewards and keep going in the right direction. We need to pick our eyes up and off our smartphones and devices to become more aware of what is going on around us. Let's ask ourselves a question: "How can I be of assistance?" Let's share the good news of our Risen Savior as joyful Easter people, our "Hallelujah" with us wherever we go!

CHAPTER 21

Rebirth in Christ Sunday

"Let us know, let us press on to know the LORD; his appearing is as sure as the dawn; he will come to us like the showers, like the spring rains that water the earth."
—Hosea 6:3

FAMILY MORNING PRAYER

Read the verse above and pray the Morning Offering together as a family.

Morning Offering: Dear Lord Jesus, thank you for the gift of today— your Sunday. Please guide our family as we strive to grow closer to you and to one another. Open our hearts and teach us to be much more generous with our time. Open our eyes to discover opportunities to love others. Amen.

Pray: *Our Father, Hail Mary, Glory Be.*

REFLECT

During the Easter season we want to be mindful that we are "the Easter people and hallelujah is our song" as St. John Paul II has told us and as I noted earlier. We have much to celebrate. Jesus died for us on the wood of the Cross to then rise from the dead on Easter Sunday! He won the victory for us. We must not get bogged down with the sufferings and the pettiness of life, but rather lovingly offer it all to Jesus and ask him to use it for his glory. He will grant graces to us. We need to ask him. In addition, try your best to open your heart wider to the graces during this special holy season. Ask God to help you to become reborn in him.

What ways do we show others that we are joyful Easter people? Ponder how you can help to make a difference in someone's life this Easter season with your loving acts of mercy and your beautiful Christian witness. Try your best on the Lord's Day to step away from the distractions of the beckoning culture. Instead, carve out the essential time for your family to be nourished in their faith and to enjoy family togetherness and a bit of rest.

CHOOSE AN ACTIVITY

Scavenger or treasure hunt: Arrange a scavenger or treasure hunt. The difference is that you will need to hide certain items that you choose to use in a treasure hunt, while there's no need to hide anything in a scavenger hunt. Recruit the older children to help you plan the games or to accompany the younger ones.

Depending upon the weather and your surroundings, you can do either game inside or outside. For the treasure hunt, make a map if you'd like, or simply a list of clues. For the scavenger hunt, plan ahead to figure out items you will ask them to find. Make a list of what they need to find, and allow them to check their list off as they do. The first person to check everything off is the winner! Perhaps the winner will receive a prize of an extra privilege or a small treat. As well, a big, warm, congratulatory hug will be a wonderful prize!

NOTE TO PARENTS AND GRANDPARENTS

Talk to the children about the need to worship together, spend time together, and get some rest. Your loving reminders will build a wonderful foundation of prayer and family Sundays.

MINI TEACHING

Why we go to Mass: We don't just go to church for Mass on Sundays when we feel like it. We participate in the holy sacrifice of the Mass because as baptized Catholics we are obligated to do so. Unless we have legitimate reasons, we need to go to Mass on Sundays (or the Saturday night vigil Mass) and on holy days (or the vigil Mass). A succinct explanation by EWTN theologian Colin B. Donovan, STL, can help our understanding. He stated, "It is both a precept of the Church and Church law that Catholics must worship God on Sunday and Holy Days of Obligation by participating in the Holy Mass." Why should we? He explains why. He said, "This follows from the fact that in the Mass it is Christ Himself who worships the Father, joining our worship to His."

Can we offer thanks in some other way and skip Mass? Donovan states, "In no other way is it possible to adequately give thanks (eucharistia) to God for the blessings of creation, redemption and our sanctification than by uniting our offerings to that of Jesus Christ Himself." He then tells us why we worship on Sundays. "Following the example of the Old Covenant the Church does this weekly, on the day of the Lord's Resurrection."[10] Discuss this teaching with the family.

PONDER

From Old English we get the word "Easter" which means "East." As the sun, which rises in the East, brings light and warmth, the Christian is reminded of Jesus rising from the dead to bring us new life—full of light and hope. Today's chapter title is "Rebirth in Christ." How can you be reborn in Christ? For this to happen, put in the time. In other words, make sure God is on your "to-do" list—right at the top! Make time for him. Learn from him! Pray to be his light in a darkened world. As well, enjoy creating special family experiences and warm memories today and throughout the Easter season.

FAMILY EVENING PRAYER
to be prayed each evening this week

Dear Lord, thank you for the blessings of this day—your day. If we have failed you in any way, please forgive us. If we have failed one another by not taking care of our responsibilities, please forgive us, Lord. Please help us to grow in holiness each day. We love you! Amen.

Pray: *Our Father, Hail Mary, Glory Be.*

Joyful Hearts Sunday

"Joy is prayer. Joy is strength. Joy is love. Joy is a net of love by which you can catch souls."
—Saint Teresa of Calcutta

FAMILY MORNING PRAYER

Read the verse above and pray the Morning Offering together as a family.

Morning Offering: Dear Lord Jesus, thank you for the gift of today—your Sunday. Please guide our family as we strive to grow closer to you and to one another. Open our hearts and teach us to be much more generous with our time. Open our eyes to discover opportunities to love others. Amen.

Pray: *Our Father, Hail Mary, Glory Be.*

REFLECT

Do you have a joyful heart? The search for happiness is universal. We all want happiness in our lives However, *joy* is not the same as happiness. Joy is stronger. It's not the "warm fuzzies" or a fleeting emotion. It's something very real and holy. Joy remains in our hearts even amid sorrow or pain, as contradictory as that might sound. Joy means achieving selflessness to the point of personal sacrifice. Mother Teresa, who often spoke about joy, left the familiar routine and happiness she felt as a principal in teaching and guiding at a girls' school in Loreto to embrace the joy in caring for the suffering bodies and souls of the forgotten and poor in Calcutta, India. Think about that. Our Lord called her. She followed. Parents and grandparents certainly have joy in their hearts even while they pray for the well-being of the children who might be in trouble. We have joy in the hope of Eternal Life. When we are one with God and connected to his people, we have joy in our hearts.

CHOOSE AN ACTIVITY

Sacred Heart of Jesus and Immaculate Heart of Mary craft: When speaking about the Sacred Heart of Jesus, Saint Margaret Mary Alacoque (1690) said, "If you only knew how much merit and glory there is in honoring this loving Heart of the adorable Jesus and how great will be the recompense for those who strive only to honor it!"[11] Even though the feasts of the Sacred Heart of Jesus and the Immaculate Heart of Mary do not fall within the Easter season, we can always honor them with love and devotion and learn more about them. As well, today we are speaking about "joyful hearts"!

Research images of the Sacred Heart of Jesus and the Immaculate Heart of Mary. Gather the kids, pencils, markers, crayons, and paper, and do your best to be artistic! Make beautiful Sacred and Immaculate Heart images that you might hang to admire and by which to become inspired. You might consider framing at least one of them.

NOTE TO PARENTS AND GRANDPARENTS

Talk to the children about being joyful. Ask them to tell you three ways that they will try to have a more positive attitude in which to listen to God and accept his holy will in their lives. Help them. Ask them how their joy can help others. Have them make a list of five ways. As always, impress upon them the need to treat Sundays in a special way, gathering around the family table to break bread together as a family. Make sure you carve out at least a little time for rest too.

MINI TEACHING

Saint Paul, when speaking about the desires of the flesh as opposed to the Spirit, preached, "By contrast, the fruit of the Spirit is love, joy, peace, patience, kindness, generosity, faithfulness, gentleness, and self-control. There is no law against such things. And those who belong to Christ

Jesus have crucified the flesh with its passions and desires. If we live by the Spirit, let us also be guided by the Spirit. Let us not become conceited, competing against one another, envying one another" (Gal. 5:22–26).

Saint Peter exclaimed, "Although you have not seen him, you love him; and even though you do not see him now, you believe in him and rejoice with an indescribable and glorious joy" (1 Pet. 1:8).

Saint James encourages us, "My brothers and sisters, whenever you face trials of any kind, consider it nothing but joy, because you know that the testing of your faith produces endurance; and let endurance have its full effect, so that you may be mature and complete, lacking in nothing" (James 1:2–4). Do we have those things St. Paul speaks of? Do we love our Lord so much—with "indescribable and glorious joy" as St. Peter describes? Do we have joy in our hearts as St. James encourages?

PONDER

Consider ways you can become more alive in your Faith and possess joy in your heart, as well as the questions above. Be sure to have fun with the family. Step back from technology as much as you can.

FAMILY EVENING PRAYER

to be prayed each evening this week

Dear Lord, thank you for the blessings of this day—your day. If we have failed you in any way, please forgive us. If we have failed one another by not taking care of our responsibilities, please forgive us, Lord. Please help us to grow in holiness each day. Please fill our hearts with your joy. We love you! Amen.

Pray: *Our Father, Hail Mary, Glory Be.*

CHAPTER 23

Easter Blessings Sunday

"And ever anew we must withdraw our hearts from the force of gravity, which pulls them down, and inwardly we must raise them high: in truth and love. At this hour, let us thank the Lord, because through the power of his word and of the holy Sacraments, he points us in the right direction and draws our heart upwards. Let us pray to him in these words: Yes, Lord, make us Easter people, men and women of light, filled with the fire of your love. Amen."
—Pope Emeritus Benedict XVI, March 22, 2008, Easter Vigil

FAMILY MORNING PRAYER

Read the verse above and pray the Morning Offering together as a family.

Morning Offering: Dear Lord Jesus, thank you for the gift of today—your Sunday. Please guide our family as we strive to grow closer to you and to one another. Open our hearts and teach us to be much more generous with our time. Open our eyes to discover opportunities to love others. Amen.

Pray: *Our Father, Hail Mary, Glory Be.*

REFLECT

During this Easter season, we are supposed to grow in holiness. Pope Emeritus Benedict XVI reminds us that we should be "Easter people" and to ask God to help us to radiate his light and love to others. He encourages us to pray, "Lord, make us Easter people, men and women of light, filled with the fire of your love. Amen." Benedict also cautioned that we must not let the "force of gravity" of the world pull us down, but rather we should raise our hearts high—seeking God's help through the power of God's word and the holy sacraments. In that way we are pointed in the right direction—to heaven and its rewards.

Think about whether or not you are truly an "Easter people." Could you possibly carve out additional time for studying the Faith and for prayer? Even a half hour's time each Sunday would be beneficial. You might consider using my book *Feeding Your Family's Soul: Dinner Table Spirituality*. Help the family to be less focused on the "force of gravity," or, in other words, on the bombardment of the culture's values or lack thereof. Making the time for Mass, prayer, and reflection will help keep everyone pointed in the right direction. Make a point of getting out to the Sacrament of Confession. Living in this way, you set a lovely and meaningful example for others.

CHOOSE AN ACTIVITY

In our teaching below we learn about the importance of transforming our home into a "domestic church." Read the mini teaching below and possibly choose to do an activity that would involve sprucing up your home—your domestic church. This could mean creating colorful pictures of Jesus, Mary, or the saints, making a simple crucifix, or getting holy items out of drawers and storage areas to dust off and display. Holy images draw our hearts heavenward.

Bedroom door welcome cross: Gather the family and arts and crafts materials. Have each family member draw a cross on construction paper and cut it out. With your help, have the children state five reasons that they are thankful that Jesus died on the cross and rose from the dead for them. Write these on their crosses. Allow the children to decorate their crosses. Before hanging their works of art on their bedroom doors (or wherever you find appropriate), have them share their sentiments.

NOTE TO PARENTS AND GRANDPARENTS

Talk to the children about the need to spend quality time with the family. By "quality," I mean without the distraction of smartphones, electronic games, and devices. Also impress upon the children that Sunday is the perfect day to get some rest. It's the Lord's Day, after all.

MINI TEACHING

Holy reminders: One way to help the family grow in Faith is to have what Mother Angelica (EWTN) would often call "holy reminders" all around us. Of course, we can be reminded of God when we look at his marvelous creation out in nature. However, we can also be reminded of the need to grow in our Faith and journey closer to God as we observe beautiful holy images around our homes, which are meant to be our "domestic churches."

The Catechism teaches: "Following the divinely inspired teaching of our holy Fathers and the tradition of the Catholic Church (for we know that this tradition comes from the Holy Spirit who dwells in her) we rightly define with full certainty and correctness that, like the figure of the precious and life-giving cross, venerable and holy images of our Lord and God and Savior, Jesus Christ, our inviolate Lady, the holy Mother of God, and the venerated angels, all the saints and the just, whether painted or made of mosaic or another suitable material, are to be exhibited in the holy churches of God, on sacred vessels and vestments, walls and panels, in houses and on streets" (CCC, no. 1161).

PONDER

Consider ways you can become more alive in your Faith. As you pray, ask God to help you to not get bogged down by the "force of gravity" of the world that Pope Emeritus Benedict XVI spoke about. Have fun creating marvelous Sunday memories for your family.

FAMILY EVENING PRAYER

to be prayed each evening this week

Dear Lord, thank you for the blessings of this day—your day. If we have failed you in any way, please forgive us. If we have failed one another by not taking care of our responsibilities, please forgive us, Lord. Please help us to grow in holiness each day. Lord, make us Easter people of light, filled with the fire of your love. Please strengthen us so that the "force of gravity" of the world will not pull us down. We love you! Amen."

Pray: *Our Father, Hail Mary, Glory Be.*

CHAPTER 24

Faith and Fun Sunday

"To believe in Jesus is to accept what he says, even when it runs contrary to what others are saying."
—Saint John Paul II, 17th World Youth Day, Toronto, July 27, 2002

FAMILY MORNING PRAYER

Read the verse above and pray the Morning Offering together as a family.

Morning Offering: Dear Lord Jesus, thank you for the gift of today—your Sunday. Please guide our family as we strive to grow closer to you and to one another. Open our hearts and teach us to be much more generous with our time. Open our eyes to discover opportunities to love others. Amen.

Pray: *Our Father, Hail Mary, Glory Be.*

REFLECT

Be countercultural! We read in Romans 12:2, "Do not be conformed to the world, but be transformed by the renewing of your minds, so that you may discern what is the will of God—what is good and acceptable and perfect." I have used words from St. John Paul II to open our chapter: "To believe in Jesus is to accept what he says, even when it runs contrary to what others are saying." The saints have lived countercultural lives and often teach us by their example and speech. I love the way that Servant of God Archbishop Fulton Sheen encouraged the faithful to lead countercultural lives. He told us not to be a "dead body"! That's right—a dead body. Specifically, he wrote:

Thirty or forty years ago it was easy to be a Christian. The very air we breathed was Christian. Bicycles could be left on front lawns; doors could be left unlocked. Suddenly, all this has changed. Now we have to affirm our faith. We live in a world that challenges us. And many fall away. Dead bodies float downstream; it takes live bodies to resist the current. And this is our summons.[12]

Let's be sure to think about whether or not we are allowing ourselves and our families to be "conformed to the world."

CHOOSE AN ACTIVITY

Family discussion: Gathered at the table for a meal, ask the family what ways they could lead countercultural lives. Start by explaining why it's important not to follow the ways of the world that are contradictory or against our Catholic Faith. List a couple of ways that our Faith teaches us to be different. Give the first example of a way in which to live in a countercultural way.

You might say that for you as a parent or grandparent, you do not allow the demands of the culture dictate how you live. Another example would be that you make sure that you get to Mass on Sunday or the Saturday night vigil, and not allow demanding sports or other schedules to get in the way.

Today is "Faith and Fun Sunday." In addition to learning more about your Faith, decide upon fun activities together and carry them out. This shouldn't be too difficult to plan. Make sure you plan plenty of time for fun activities. Play, play, play!

NOTE TO PARENTS AND GRANDPARENTS

Talk to the children about the continual need to cut back on extra technology today, and in addition to spending time together, and reaching out in service to someone who needs help, to get rest, too, so that you can become refreshed and start the new week with vim and vigor!

MINI TEACHING

Read this quote to prepare your heart: "It was pride that changed angels into devils. It is humility that makes men as angels" —Saint Augustine. Ponder ways that you might be tempted to pride. You might ask yourself a few questions:

Do you want to continually prove yourself to others?

Can you allow others to voice their opinions without interrupting?

Can you strive to be more cognizant of the temptations to be prideful?

Can you take time each day to say a prayer for humility and ask God forgiveness for the times you are prideful?

Do you strive to live out your Faith?

Are you countercultural? Can you be?

After answering these questions yourself, ask the children. Help them with their answers. Ask them, based on their reflections, to put at least one resolution into practice this coming week. This will help them to seek humility rather than to be prideful.

PONDER

Think about Servant of God Archbishop Fulton Sheen's words, "We live in a world that challenges us. And many fall away. Dead bodies float downstream; it takes live bodies to resist the current. And this is our summons." How are you challenged by the world's values or lack thereof? What can you do to be sure that you will not become a "dead body"? As well, how might your faithful and vibrant example help others who have abandoned their faith and those thinking about leaving the Church?

FAMILY EVENING PRAYER

to be prayed each evening this week

Dear Lord, thank you for the blessings of this day—your day. If we have failed you in any way, please forgive us. If we have failed one another by not taking care of our responsibilities, please forgive us, Lord. Please help us to grow in holiness each day. Help us to be mindful of the evil influences of the world. We love you! Amen.

Pray: *Our Father, Hail Mary, Glory Be.*

Advent Sundays

"The liturgy of Advent, filled with constant allusions to the joyful expectation of the Messiah, helps us to understand the fullness of the value and meaning of the mystery of Christmas. It is not just about commemorating the historical event, which occurred some 2,000 years ago in a little village of Judea. Instead, we must understand that our whole life should be an 'advent', in vigilant expectation of Christ's final coming. To prepare our hearts to welcome the Lord who, as we say in the Creed, will come one day to judge the living and the dead, we must learn to recognize his presence in the events of daily life. Advent is then a period of intense training that directs us decisively to the One who has already come, who will come and who continuously comes."
—Saint John Paul II, General Audience, December 18, 2002

I n her marvelous wisdom, the Church gifts us with a special liturgical season in which to prepare our hearts. Advent really has a twofold purpose. We are to prepare our hearts for the coming of the Christ Child. But, in addition, we prepare for the Second Coming of Christ. Advent is a season of hope and expectation. We anticipate grace and the coming of God into our hearts—the God who humbled himself to be born a little baby, not in a palace, but rather in a smelly manger where the breath of animals helped to keep him warm.

We have much to ponder in the Advent season. We should strive to carve out additional time for prayer and studying the

Faith. Perhaps, most importantly, to try to slow down, step away from the prevalent advertising frenzy, pause, and allow our Lord to speak to our hearts. Ponder why our Lord, who is God, came to us as a small child. Pray to become more humble this Advent.

⤴ CHAPTER 25 ⤵

Patiently Waiting Sunday

"*Mary,* who in this novena of preparation for Christmas, guides us toward Bethlehem. Mary is the *Woman of the "yes"* who, contrary to Eve, makes the plan of God her own without reservation. Thus she becomes a *clear light* for our steps and *the highest model* for our inspiration."
—Saint John Paul II, General Audience, December 18, 2002

FAMILY MORNING PRAYER

Read the verse above and pray the Morning Offering together as a family.

Morning Offering: Dear Lord Jesus, thank you for the gift of today—your Sunday. Please guide our family as we strive to grow closer to you and to one another. Open our hearts and teach us to be much more generous with our time. Open our eyes to discover opportunities to love others. Amen.

Pray: *Our Father, Hail Mary, Glory Be.*

REFLECT

The holy season of Advent is all about waiting. We are waiting for Christmas, the birth of the Christ Child. However, we are also reminded to await the Second Coming of Christ. Saint John Paul II reminds us that we need to pay attention and recognize God's presence within the events of our lives. Specifically, he said, "To prepare our hearts to welcome the Lord who, as we say in the Creed, will come one day to judge the living and the dead, we must learn to recognize his presence in the events of daily life. Advent is then a period of intense training that directs us decisively to the One who has already come, who will come and who continuously comes" (Saint John Paul II, from that same General Audience, December 18, 2002).

This time of year can seem pretty chaotic because of the advertising bombardment that is difficult to escape. However, we need to do our best to retreat to the quiet (wherever that may be!). If it's not possible to find a quiet place in which to offer your heart to God, do your best to try to quiet your mind and heart and listen to our Lord speaking to your soul. Lift your heart to God often throughout the day. Today's chapter title is "Patiently Waiting Sunday." Do your best to wait patiently, delve more deeply into your Faith, and pray more earnestly. Try to set a prayerful and joyful tone around your domestic church.

CHOOSE AN ACTIVITY

Learn about the Blessed Mother: Perhaps, you might choose to read something about the Blessed Mother from the Catechism or from a book from your personal library.

Read Scripture: One suggestion is to read aloud to the family Luke 2:1–20. Ask the family to listen to the words and imagine being in that wondrous scene. In addition, check the back of this book for further activity ideas.

NOTE TO PARENTS AND GRANDPARENTS

Talk to the children about praying more often and being patient with one another. This season is about prayerfully and patiently waiting with great hope in our hearts. Make sure you open your heart to God's graces in this holy season, and do not allow the noise of the world to drown out your efforts or his voice.

MINI TEACHING

The Blessed Mother Mary has much to teach us. Saint John Paul II tells us that during Advent, Mary "guides us toward Bethlehem." Mary, as the new Eve, "makes the plan of God her own without reservation. Thus she becomes a *clear light* for our steps and *the highest model* for our inspiration." We can always count on Mary to lead us to her Son, Jesus. We recall that she told the wine stewards to "Do whatever he tells you." We can be absolutely certain that as we pray and get to know Mother Mary better, she will assuredly be a "*clear light*" to our path and "*the highest model* for our inspiration*," as Saint John Paul II has expressed.

PONDER

As you pray, allow God to make you new, so you will be an exemplary Christian example to your family and others. Have fun with your family and thank God for the amazing blessing of family!

FAMILY EVENING PRAYER

to be prayed each evening this week

Dear Lord, thank you for the blessings of this day—your day. If we have failed you in any way, please forgive us. If we have failed one another by not taking care of our responsibilities, please forgive us, Lord. Please help us to grow in holiness each day. We love you! Amen.

Pray: *Our Father, Hail Mary, Glory Be.*

CHAPTER 26

Stepping Back Sunday

"In this season of Advent, the invitation of the Prophet Isaiah accompanies us: 'Say to those who are fearful of heart. Be strong, fear not! Behold, your God . . . will come and save you.' (Is. 35:4). It becomes more urgent as Christmas approaches, enriched with the exhortation to prepare our hearts to welcome the Messiah. The one awaited by the people will certainly come and his salvation will be for all."
—Saint John Paul II, General Audience, December 18, 2002

FAMILY MORNING PRAYER

Read the verse above and pray the Morning Offering together as a family.

Morning Offering: Dear Lord Jesus, thank you for the gift of today—your Sunday. Please guide our family as we strive to grow closer to you and to one another. Open our hearts and teach us to be much more generous with our time. Open our eyes to discover opportunities to love others. Amen.

Pray: *Our Father, Hail Mary, Glory Be.*

REFLECT

While journeying through Advent, we are called to get our hearts ready to greet the Christ Child, as well as to prepare for Christ's Second Coming. What could this mean to you personally? Ponder that. This holy season is the perfect time to step back from the busy holiday distractions that call for your attention. Try your best to create an atmosphere of calm and holiness in your domestic church. Consider using an Advent wreath throughout Advent and lighting a candle at the dinner table when you pray together. You might want to use an Advent devotional. Whatever means you decide to use to grow in holiness, strive to delve deeper into your Faith, spending less time on secular things. This is a time to step away from novels and senseless secular media. Instead, immerse yourself more fully into the holiness of the season.

CHOOSE AN ACTIVITY

Stepping back: Today is about making a point to step back—step back from technology as best as you can. This will hopefully provide a quieter atmosphere in which you can pray, have conversations, and actually hear yourself think! But, also, try to "step back" in time! Take out the family photo albums or even videos, and reminisce about earlier times, especially if you have photos of older generations. Take the time to talk about their lives—what they meant to you and perhaps their favorite things to do. Share your memories. You might even consider researching your family tree. That will be an ongoing project. Talk about that possibility tonight at the dinner table.

Time capsule: Plan to make a time capsule with your family. Would you put a dated note inside along with some pertinent items? Where would you put it? Would you bury it? Even if you won't carry this out, it will be fun to spend time planning it. Ask each family member what they could add to the capsule that would represent their personality.

NOTE TO PARENTS AND GRANDPARENTS

Talk to the children about the need to refrain from senseless television viewing, reminding them also that Sunday is a special day to enjoy together. If possible, all of the family should try to get a bit of rest, too, to be refreshed on Sunday—the Lord's Day. You'll go into the new week with renewed energy. At least, that is the hope!

MINI TEACHING

Pausing: Our modern lives seem to keep us involved in a whirlwind of activity. Even at home, at times we seem to be racing against the clock, or we might feel the need to keep busy—almost as if it's a sin to be still! It's hard to escape this compulsion to keep busy all the time. And it's not just the younger generations. Adults get caught up too. Part of the problem is that everything seems to go very fast, particularly technology. Social media is all about speed. We can become conditioned to listen for every single "ding" that alerts us to a new status update.

Yet, to really experience life in every moment, we need to learn to pause. We have to be quiet. We should be listening for God. Pope Francis once cautioned, "Pause from this compulsion to a fast-paced life that scatters, divides and ultimately destroys time with family, with friends, with children, with grandparents, and time as a gift" (Ash Wednesday Homily, February 14, 2018). This might sound paradoxical, but work hard at developing a "pausing habit." Teach the family the importance of not getting caught up in the noise and busyness of the culture. Train the family to pause and take the time to listen to God instead. Form at least three habits of pausing throughout your days. This could be morning, noon, and night, to take at least five minutes of time to pause, ponder, and pray. You can do it!

PONDER

Try to be more attentive this Advent season—attentive to God and to the needs of others around you. How will you serve God and others? Strive to pause from busyness on a regular basis. It is good for the heart and soul!

FAMILY EVENING PRAYER
to be prayed each evening this week

Dear Lord, thank you for the blessings of this day—your day. If we have failed you in any way, please forgive us. If we have failed one another by not taking care of our responsibilities, please forgive us, Lord. Please help us to grow in holiness each day. We love you! Amen.

Pray: *Our Father, Hail Mary, Glory Be.*

Saints for Advent Sunday

"The season of Advent restores . . . a hope which does not disappoint for it is founded on God's Word. A hope which does not disappoint, simply because the Lord never disappoints! . . . Let us think about and feel this beauty."

—Pope Francis, Sunday Angelus, December 1, 2013

FAMILY MORNING PRAYER

Read the verse above and pray the Morning Offering together as a family.

Morning Offering: Dear Lord Jesus, thank you for the gift of today—your Sunday. Please guide our family as we strive to grow closer to you and to one another. Open our hearts and teach us to be much more generous with our time. Open our eyes to discover opportunities to love others. Amen.

Pray: *Our Father, Hail Mary, Glory Be.*

REFLECT

The saints have much to teach us. We are blessed to be part of the great communion of saints, and we can call upon the saints in heaven anytime to request their intercession for us. As well, we can learn from their lives of holiness, keeping in mind that the saints were once a "work in progress" just like ourselves. Saints were not born with sparkling halos hovering over their heads. Once we realize that fact, and let it sink into our brains, we might not be so hesitant to work hard at our own sanctity, knowing that if they could do it, then we can do it too!

Talk to the family about the saints. Choose an Advent saint to learn about. Do a little research from an approved source, and read at least a few paragraphs to the family. Here are some ideas. Extra "points" for you if you can come up with more!

The Blessed Mother (because she is the Mother of Jesus!)

Saint Joseph (because he is the foster father of Jesus and the husband of Mary)

Saint Nicholas (otherwise known as Santa Claus!)

Saint Thérèse of Lisieux (for her love of the Child Jesus)

Saint Teresa of Ávila (for her love of Saint Joseph, who is part of the Holy Family)

Saint John the Baptist (who tells us to prepare the way of the Lord)

Saint Lucy (whose feast day is December 13)

Saint John of the Cross (whose feast day is December 14)

Saint Francis of Assisi, who set up the first Nativity scene in Greccio, Italy, in AD 1223.)

CHOOSE AN ACTIVITY

Perhaps you will choose an activity that is related to a saint—drawing saint pictures, reading a saint's story, setting up a manger, or making a recipe relating to a saint.

Make a saints' trivia game: Collect saint prayer cards. Perhaps you have a collection already. Glue them on pieces of bright construction paper (all the same color). You are making a deck of saint cards. After making these, have fun with it during trivia games! At the breakfast table, have the children draw a saint card from the deck but keep it a secret about who their saint is. You (the parent or grandparent) should make a mental note or write it down. After everyone has had a turn choosing a card, place the cards back in the deck. Sometime throughout the day (with your help or an older sibling's help), the children should research at least three facts about their saint. At the dinner table, you'll play the saint trivia game. Each child mentions the saint facts out loud—one at a time (without revealing the saint)—and the others will try to guess the saint. Have fun!

NOTE TO PARENTS AND GRANDPARENTS

Talk to the children about the need to be more patient with one another. Let them know you understand it's sometimes difficult to be patient, and sometimes you have trouble yourself. Tell them that even the saints had trouble, but they worked hard to persevere in being good. We are all works in progress and need to pray for help to grow in virtue. As well, the old saying "practice makes perfect" certainly comes into play.

MINI TEACHING

Saint Faustina was a humble and prayerful Polish nun who was entrusted with a great mission by God to spread the devotion of Divine Mercy. Jesus appeared to her several times and gave her many teachings about Divine Mercy. He told her that we must admit our need for his mercy and humble ourselves to receive it. In that way, we will be able to offer mercy to others.

Jesus told St. Faustina that there are three ways to offer mercy: by deed, word, or prayer:

> You are to show mercy to your neighbors always and everywhere. You must not shrink from this or try to excuse or abstain from it. I am giving you three ways of exercising mercy toward your neighbor: first—by deed, second—by word, third—by prayer. In these three acts is contained the fullness of mercy, and it is an unquestionable demonstration of love for Me. By this means a soul glorifies and pays reverence to My mercy.[13]

Talk to the family about the need to show God's mercy to others. Help the children understand that God wants us always to be merciful. Ask them to help you plan ways to show mercy to your neighbors and anyone in need. List the ideas on paper, and work at carrying them out.

PONDER

Take time to consider ways you can become more alive in your Faith by expressing it to others in deeds, words, and prayers. Take time for playing and laughing! All the while, believe it or not, you are actually working out your salvation and creating memories for your family!

FAMILY EVENING PRAYER
to be prayed each evening this week

Dear Lord, thank you for the blessings of this day—your day. If we have failed you in any way, please forgive us. If we have failed one another by not taking care of our responsibilities, please forgive us, Lord. Please help us to grow in holiness each day. We love you! Amen.

Pray: *Our Father, Hail Mary, Glory Be.*

✑ CHAPTER 28 ✑

Preparing Our Hearts Sunday

"If you direct your heart rightly, you will
stretch out your hands toward him."
—Job 11:13

FAMILY MORNING PRAYER

Read the verse above and pray the Morning Offering together as a family.

Morning Offering: Dear Lord Jesus, thank you for the gift of today—
your Sunday. Please guide our family as we strive to grow closer to you
and to one another. Open our hearts and teach us to be much more
generous with our time. Open our eyes to discover opportunities to love
others. Amen.

Pray: *Our Father, Hail Mary, Glory Be.*

REFLECT

Today is "Preparing our Hearts Sunday." Make it all about preparing
your heart to meet the Christ Child at Christmas, as well as being ready
to meet Our Lord at his Second Coming or when you depart from this
life. That might sound a tad morbid, but it is not at all. Death is really an
important part of our lives for it is when we are ushered into Eternal Life!
Mother Teresa called it "our Coronation."

In order to prepare your heart and help your family to prepare theirs,
you will want to deepen your Faith. How can you do that? With prayer
and with study. Sunday is the perfect day to learn more about your Faith;
that will please God, thus preparing your heart even just a bit more to be
ready to greet him.

CHOOSE AN ACTIVITY

Short Catechism lesson: Consider opening the Catechism of the Catholic Church or look up a category from the Catechism online. Choose a subject and read a few paragraphs, and convey it to the family. Feel free to ask the children a few questions about what you have taught them. A fifteen-minute to half-hour learning activity can be foundational to your children's lives.

Heart craft: You might want to do a craft involving hearts—even simply drawing colorful hearts. Take it a step further and have the children write a message on each heart about how they will carry out a work of mercy soon. Cut the hearts out and decorate a bulletin board, the refrigerator, or hang them on an arts and crafts "clothesline."

Perhaps you will choose to make a fun recipe together—possibly even Christmas cookies. Or, possibly, you'll make heart cookies! It's not Valentine's Day, but it is "Preparing our Hearts Sunday!" Plan on making extra cookies, and gift them to someone who would enjoy them. If they are surprised about heart cookies, rather than Christmas cookies, you'll have a perfect opportunity to share that you are preparing your hearts for Jesus!

NOTE TO PARENTS AND GRANDPARENTS

Talk to the children about the need to love others as God has loved us. Encourage them to get along well with their family members and friends. If they feel that they want to argue or try too hard to get their point across, ask them to pause and say a little prayer for peace.

MINI TEACHING

A famous priest's sharing his love for Mary through teaching the prayer of the Rosary might have had its beginnings when a simple priest from Ireland helped a potato farmer with his crop and noticed that the family lacked the family prayer that he was taught by his own family. Because of his sharing, they began to pray the family Rosary every night. This priest was Father Patrick Peyton, csc, now famously known for his statement, "The family that prays together, stays together." He would go on to found the "Family Rosary Crusade."

Have you begun praying a family Rosary? It might seem daunting, but it is a powerful family prayer. Even a decade a day is very beneficial. If you can pray a five-decade Rosary, take turns leading the decades. Offer the Rosary for families all around the world and any specific needs. The Blessed Mother at Fatima asked that we pray a daily Rosary for peace in the world. Father Peyton's encouragement helps us. He said, "If families give Our Lady fifteen minutes a day by reciting the Rosary, I assure them that their homes will become by God's grace, peaceful places." What about sacred images in your home? Do you strive to make your abode into a domestic church? As well, do you partake in the sacraments and liturgical celebrations? Here are a few things to consider:

Is there a crucifix in every bedroom of your domestic church?

How about other sacred images throughout your home?

Could you add an image of the Sacred Heart of Jesus and the Immaculate Heart of Mary in a prominent place in your home?

Do you schedule regular times for Confession—perhaps on First Saturdays? Take the whole family.

Consider beginning family traditions based on liturgical seasons.

PONDER

Take time to ponder ways in which you can become more alive in your Faith and prepare your heart more lovingly for the Lord. Have fun with the family, and through your loving activities, prayers, and teachings impress upon them the joy and blessing of family.

FAMILY EVENING PRAYER
to be prayed each evening this week

Dear Lord, thank you for the blessings of this day—your day. If we have failed you in any way, please forgive us. If we have failed one another by not taking care of our responsibilities, please forgive us, Lord. Please help us to grow in holiness each day. We love you! Amen.

Pray: *Our Father, Hail Mary, Glory Be.*

Marian Sundays

"Mary's role in the Church is inseparable from her union with Christ and flows directly from it. 'This union of the mother with the Son in the work of salvation is made manifest from the time of Christ's virginal conception up to his death'; it is made manifest above all at the hour of his Passion:

Thus the Blessed Virgin advanced in her pilgrimage of faith, and faithfully persevered in her union with her Son unto the cross. There she stood, in keeping with the divine plan, enduring with her only begotten Son the intensity of his suffering, joining herself with his sacrifice in her mother's heart, and lovingly consenting to the immolation of this victim, born of her: to be given, by the same Christ Jesus dying on the cross, as a mother to his disciple, with these words: 'Woman, behold your son.'"
—CCC, no. 964

T he Church teaches that the Blessed Virgin Mary's role is directly related to her union with her Son Jesus Christ, the one who started the Church: "By her complete adherence to the Father's will, to his Son's redemptive work, and to every prompting of the Holy Spirit, the Virgin Mary is the Church's model of faith and charity. Thus she is a 'preeminent and . . . wholly unique member of the Church'; indeed, she is the 'exemplary realization' (*typus*) of the Church"

(CCC, no. 967). In addition, the Catechism explains Mary's holy and wholehearted cooperation with grace and her particular role as "a mother to us in the order of grace." Specifically, we learn, "Her role in relation to the Church and to all humanity goes still further. 'In a wholly singular way she cooperated by her obedience, faith, hope, and burning charity in the Savior's work of restoring supernatural life to souls. For this reason she is a mother to us in the order of grace'" (CCC, no. 968 and *Lumen Gentium*, no. 6).

We should be assured that Mother Mary is not just resting on her throne in heaven! She works tirelessly and awaits our prayers! We might fear approaching her, thinking she wouldn't understand our problems. However, she is close by and always available to assist, ever since her fiat at the Annunciation. The Church teaches, "This motherhood of Mary in the order of grace continues uninterruptedly from the consent which she loyally gave at the Annunciation and which she sustained without wavering beneath the cross, until the eternal fulfillment of all the elect. Taken up to heaven she did not lay aside this saving office but by her manifold intercession continues to bring us the gifts of eternal salvation. . . . Therefore the Blessed Virgin is invoked in the Church under the titles of Advocate, Helper, Benefactress, and Mediatrix" (CCC, no. 969, and *Lumen Gentium*, no. 62). Let us never fear to approach Mother Mary in our prayers. She is our "Advocate, Helper, Benefactress, and Mediatrix."

Mary Crowning Sunday

"Hail, holy Queen, Mother of mercy, hail, our life, our sweetness
and our hope."
—from the "Hail, Holy Queen" prayer

FAMILY MORNING PRAYER

Read the verse above and pray the Morning Offering together as a family.

Morning Offering: Dear Lord Jesus, thank you for the gift of today—
your Sunday. Please guide our family as we strive to grow closer to you
and to one another. Open our hearts and teach us to be much more
generous with our time. Open our eyes to discover opportunities to love
others. Amen.

Pray: *Our Father, Hail Mary, Glory Be.*

REFLECT

We should honor Mary in our hearts and our homes. Honoring Mary is
not the same as worshiping her. We reserve worship for our Lord. Love
for and devotion to the Blessed Mother Mary were evident from the earliest days of the Church. Since today is "Mary Crowning Sunday," we
will discuss a bit of background, though it's difficult to pinpoint exactly
how the crowning of Mary originated. The fifth decade of the Glorious
mysteries of the Rosary is entitled "The Coronation of Mary: Queen of
Heaven and Earth."

With regard to Mary's crowning, in the earliest kinds of iconography
in the first century, we see that Mary and Jesus wore gold crowns,
especially in the Eastern churches. We can surmise that in most places,
the crowning of Mary (statues) occurs during the month of May, perhaps

because there are several important Marian feast days in May. Specifically, they are these: "Our Lady, Queen of Apostles" (the Saturday following Ascension); "Our Lady of the Most Blessed Sacrament" (May 13); "Our Lady of Fatima" (May 13); "Mary, Help of Christians" (May 24); "Mary, Mediatrix of All Graces" (May 31); and "The Visitation" (May 31).

You might wonder why this particular Sunday is dedicated to a Mary crowning. That is because Mary deserves to be crowned at any time— not just during the month of May! Since Mary is Queen of Heaven and Earth, she should certainly be the Queen of our hearts! To foster this belief, we can teach our families to pray the daily Rosary. We can make a special shrine or garden to Mother Mary outside in our yards. We can do a Mary crowning on any day, not just in the month of May! Mother Mary loves us and will always draw us closer to her Son Jesus.

CHOOSE AN ACTIVITY

Mary crowning: Gather children and art supplies and create pictures of the Blessed Mother wearing a crown. If it would be helpful, research a few images online and show the children. As well, make a crown out of construction paper, pipe cleaners, flowers (either real or silk), or any other suitable materials. Talk about and plan your Mary crowing "ceremony."

> Do you have a statue of Mary?
>
> How will you do the crowning?
>
> Will there be a procession of sorts? Carrying flowers to the statue of Mary?
>
> Will you play a Marian hymn or sing a song to the Blessed Mother?
>
> What prayers will you say together?
>
> Will the children take turns crowning Mary?

NOTE TO PARENTS AND GRANDPARENTS

Talk to the children about the need to treat Sunday as a special day apart from all other days of the week. Today we can focus on Mother Mary, who always draws us closer to her Son. Encourage the children to invite Mary to be with you all as you spend Sunday family time together. She is certainly with you as you worship God at Mass, pray, play, and even while you get the rest necessary to be refreshed. Encourage the children to spend time in their thoughts and prayers with Mary today and to crown her as the Queen of their hearts.

MINI TEACHING

The month of May, which is the typical month for a crowning of Mary, is a popular month for Mary's apparitions! In 1830, the Blessed Mother appeared to Saint Catherine Laboure at the motherhouse in Paris and instructed her to have the Miraculous Medal struck with the inscription, "Mary, conceived without sin, pray for us who have recourse to thee." The medal would indeed prove to be "miraculous," as many graces and favors were bestowed by Mary through her medal.

In 1846, the Blessed Mother appeared to the children of La Salette, France, and through tears, expressed her sorrow about the lax practices by the faithful. In 1858, Mary appeared to Saint Bernadette at Lourdes, France, telling the young Bernadette that she was the "Immaculate Conception." In addition, the Blessed Mother appeared to three young shepherd children (two of whom are now canonized saints) at Fatima, Portugal, on May 13, 1917, where she called for penance, asked for the Five First Saturdays devotion, and requested the daily Rosary for peace in the world. But your crowning of Mary can occur any time that you would like—not only in May.

PONDER

Can Mother Mary help you become more alive in your Faith? I believe that she can. Strive to get to know her better. Have fun with the family. It's essential to make room for playing and laughing! We can be sure that Mother Mary laughed with Saint Joseph and her precious Son, Jesus.

FAMILY EVENING PRAYER

to be prayed each evening this week

Dear Lord, thank you for the blessings of this day—your day. If we have failed you in any way, please forgive us. If we have failed one another by not taking care of our responsibilities, please forgive us, Lord. Please help us to grow in holiness each day. We love you! Amen.

Pray: *Our Father, Hail Mary, Glory Be.*

CHAPTER 30

Apparition Sunday

"As the Mother of God, the Virgin Mary has a unique position among the saints, indeed, among all creatures. She is exalted, yet still one of us."

—United States Conference of Catholic Bishops[14]

FAMILY MORNING PRAYER

Read the verse above and pray the Morning Offering together as a family.

Morning Offering: Dear Lord Jesus, thank you for the gift of today—your Sunday. Please guide our family as we strive to grow closer to you and to one another. Open our hearts and teach us to be much more generous with our time. Open our eyes to discover opportunities to love others. Amen.

Pray: *Our Father, Hail Mary, Glory Be.*

REFLECT

Parents and grandparents have received a very special entrusting from God. They are called to impart the Faith to the children from a young age. As I have mentioned throughout this book, their homes, or domestic churches, should mirror the big Church. Parents and grandparents should create an atmosphere for learning the Catholic Faith.

In my book *Our Lady's Messages to the Three Shepherd Children and the World*, Father Andrew Apostoli, CFR, world-renowned Fatima expert (now deceased), expressed the need to teach the Faith to our children and grandchildren at a young age. He said in a "Note to Parents, Grandparents, Teachers, and Guardians":

[I]t was as a child that I myself first heard about the message of Our Lady of Fatima. I saw one of the first movies about the Fatima events, and it left an impression on me all through my years of growing up. I never forgot it. Remember that little Jacinta who was probably the most zealous of the visionaries, was only six years old when the Angel of Peace appeared to the children and was only seven when Our Lady appeared to them. Surely the message made a profound impact on her. It has been said that if an idea is impressed on the mind and heart of children before the age of seven, they will never forget it. We need to bring our children to Mary at a tender age so that, as Jacinta, our Blessed Mother's message may have a profound impact on them and guide them throughout their formative years.[15]

CHOOSE AN ACTIVITY

Apparitions: Today is the perfect day to teach the family about Church-approved apparitions. In our last chapter I discussed four Church-approved apparitions: Our Lady of Fatima, Our Lady of Lourdes, Our Lady of the Miraculous Medal, and Our Lady of La Salette. There are other Church-approved apparitions, but I mentioned those four because I was discussing the month of May.

Choose one of the apparitions that I just mentioned and research and convey it to the children. Or, perhaps you would like to focus on Our Lady of Guadalupe or Our Lady of Knock, or do some research to learn about the others.

Craft: Have fun doing a craft project about Mary. Or, have the children create greeting cards with art supplies. Choose verses about the Blessed Mother from prayers or Catholic teaching, and write them on the cards. The children can write their own words about Mary. Share your Faith and gift the cards to family, neighbors, and friends!

Mary meal: What did Mary cook for Saint Joseph and Jesus? Ask the children if they can guess. They might mention fish since Jesus hung out with fishermen! Or, perhaps they will remember the loaves and fishes. Research the common food eaten at the time of the Holy Family of Nazareth, and make a meal in honor of them. Here are some foods that might be included: unleavened bread, chickpeas, dried fruits, figs, grapes, wheat, barley, olives or olive oil, lentils, black-eyed peas, lamb, poultry, wild field greens, pomegranate, soft or sour cheeses, mushrooms, honey, wine, hyssop. Possibly, goose, duck, cattle, sheep, peas, carrots, garlic. This list of foods might get you thinking of something you can whip up! If you don't make a meal, take some time to discuss the Holy Family's meals and their way of life.

NOTE TO PARENTS AND GRANDPARENTS

Talk to the children about the Blessed Mother in their lives. Focus on one of the Marian apparitions, and explain to the children that the Blessed Mother cares about every single one of her children. She wants them all safe in heaven one day. Sometimes God the Father sends Mary to earth to impress upon the world that they need to turn away from sin and embrace God's teachings. Encourage the children to reach out to Mother Mary often in prayer. She understands all of our deepest concerns and will always help us to find our way to heaven.

MINI TEACHING

The Catholic Church has always taught that everything that God the Father revealed for our salvation was revealed in the Word, Jesus Christ, who then communicated everything to his apostles, who in turn wrote it down or handed it on through their preaching (Tradition). The teachings revealed by God the Father are called "the deposit of Faith" (1 Cor. 15:1–3, 2 Thess. 2:15). We believe that we find these truths in public revelation, Sacred Scripture, and Sacred (Apostolic) Tradition.

There is also something called "private revelations" that are never necessary for our salvation and that we are not required to believe. They do not add anything more to "public revelation." Yet, the Church-approved private revelations are to help us. For instance, there have been times throughout salvation history when God sent the Mother of God to earth to wake us up from our complacency and to request prayer and penance.

According to Colin Donovan, STL, "A private revelation may recall wayward individuals to the faith, stir the devotion of the already pious, encourage prayer and penance on behalf of others, but it cannot substitute for the Catholic faith, the sacraments and hierarchical communion with the Pope and bishops."[16] There are Church-approved apparitions and there are also alleged apparitions that have not yet received the approval of the Church, as well as those supposed "apparitions" that have been condemned.

We should not chase after signs and wonders. We should be patient and wait on the Church's decision about whether or not a supposed apparition is authentic. Colin Donovan, STL, gives us pointers. He said, "The first responsibility of the faithful is to remain firmly established in the faith, in the sacraments and in communion with the Pope and bishops." That is essential. Donovan cautions, "Any Catholic who gives their primary attention to alleged private revelation at the expense of Sacred Scripture, the teaching of the Church (especially the *Catechism*), sacramental practice, prayer and fidelity to Church authority is *off course*." We should not profess to be holier than the Church or to become greedy for prophecies or revelations. Donovan added, "The running after *spiritual phenomena*, such as alleged revelations, is condemned by St. John of the Cross as spiritual avarice."[17]

PONDER

Take time to ponder Mother Mary in your life. Do you pray to her often? Why or why not? Be sure to have fun with the family—all the while striving for a peaceful atmosphere in your domestic church. Do all that you can to reclaim every Sunday. You'll be setting valuable traditions and pleasing God at the same time!

FAMILY EVENING PRAYER
to be prayed each evening this week

Dear Lord, thank you for the blessings of this day—your day. If we have failed you in any way, please forgive us. If we have failed one another by not taking care of our responsibilities, please forgive us, Lord. Please help us to grow in holiness each day. We love you! Amen.

Pray: *Our Father, Hail Mary, Glory Be.*

CHAPTER 31

Mary, Our Mother Sunday

"When the little maid of Nazareth uttered her fiat to the message of the angel . . . she became not only the Mother of God in the physical order of nature, but also in the supernatural order of grace she became the Mother of all who . . . would be made one under the Headship of her divine Son. The Mother of the Head would be the Mother of the members. The Mother of the vine would be the Mother of the branches."

—Pope Pius XII, message to the Marian Congress of Ottawa, Canada, June 19, 1947

FAMILY MORNING PRAYER

Read the verse above and pray the Morning Offering together as a family.

Morning Offering: Dear Lord Jesus, thank you for the gift of today— your Sunday. Please guide our family as we strive to grow closer to you and to one another. Open our hearts and teach us to be much more generous with our time. Open our eyes to discover opportunities to love others. Amen.

Pray: *Our Father, Hail Mary, Glory Be.*

REFLECT

What does it mean to us to have a Mother in heaven? And, not just *any* mother—but, I am talking about THE MOTHER of GOD! She is truly our Mother. She is most concerned with our spiritual well-being and intercedes for us to get to heaven at the appointed time. She works tirelessly to save souls. Her love for us is as pure as pure can be.

How did she become our Mother? When Jesus was dying on the Cross, he called out to his disciple John, who was standing near his Mother, Mary, and said, "Behold, your mother." Jesus was speaking to all his disciples to the end of time—to all of us. He also called out to his Mother, Mary, and said, "Behold, your son." Saint John Paul II spoke about Mary's motherhood when he explained,

> By her divine motherhood Mary fully opened her heart to Christ, and in him to all humanity. Mary's total dedication to the work of the Son is especially shown by her participation in his sacrifice. According to John's testimony, the Mother of Jesus "stood by the cross" (Jn 19:25). She thus united herself to all the sufferings that Jesus endured. She shared in the generous offering of his sacrifice for the salvation of mankind. (General Audience, Wednesday, April 29, 1998)

Ponder the meaning of Mary's sacrificial love and the fact that Jesus has given you the incredible gift of his Mother.

CHOOSE AN ACTIVITY

Talk about Mary: Since today is "Mary, Our Mother Sunday," take time to learn more about her. Emphasize to the children that Mother Mary loves them very much and wants them safely in heaven one day with her, and her Son, Jesus, God the Father, and the Holy Spirit, angels, and saints.

Did you know that Mary has countless titles? Among them are Blessed Among Women, Cause of Our Joy, Chosen Before Ages, Comforter of the Afflicted, Gate of Heaven, Full of Grace, Handmaid of the Lord, Holy Queen, Holy Virgin Mary, Sanctuary of the Holy Spirit, Holy Virgin, Hope of Christians, Mystical Rose, Our Lady of Sorrows, Queen of Heaven, Immaculate Conception, Immaculate Mother, Lady of Mercy, Mary, Queen of Angels, Mary, Star of the Sea, Mother of Good Counsel, Vessel of Honor, Virgin Most Pure, Woman, Clothed with the Sun, and many, many more!

Illustrate: Choose one or two of the titles of Mary and ask the children to illustrate what they think the title might mean. For help, feel free to research the titles online or a book in your personal library.

Tell a story about Mary: Ask the children to tell you the story about the Blessed Mother Mary. Help them. You can refer to Scripture or a saint's story about her.

Pray to Mary: Talk to Mary as a child would speak to their mother. Hopefully, you do this on a regular basis.

Visit a shrine to Mary: Though you might need to plan this in advance, visiting a Marian Shrine is educational and spiritually rewarding. As well, there could be an indulgence attached to it, depending upon the circumstances. Ask your parish priest about that.

NOTE TO PARENTS AND GRANDPARENTS

Talk to the children about the Mother of God. Pray at least three extra Hail Marys together for a special intention. Reinforce the need to spend time together, undistracted. You can ask Mother Mary to help you to achieve this.

MINI TEACHING

We learn about Mother Mary's being united to her Son, Jesus, in sacrifice and her universal motherhood from St. John Paul II:

> This association with Christ's sacrifice brought about a new motherhood in Mary. She who suffered for all men became the mother of all men. Jesus himself proclaimed this new motherhood when he said to her from the height of the cross: "Woman, behold, your son" (Jn 19:26). Mary thus became the mother of the beloved disciple and, in Jesus' intention, the mother of every disciple, every Christian.

Mary's universal motherhood, intended to foster life according to the Spirit, is an extraordinary gift to humanity from Christ crucified. Jesus said to the beloved disciple: "Behold, your mother". And from that hour he "took her to his own home" (Jn 19:27), or better, "among his possessions", among the precious gifts left him by the crucified Master.

The words, 'Behold, your mother', are addressed to each of us. We are invited to love Mary as Christ loved her, to welcome her into our lives as our Mother, to let her lead us along the ways of the Holy Spirit. (General Audience, Wednesday, April 29, 1998)

PONDER

Think about Mother Mary's role in your life. Ask her to help you find ways in which you can become more alive in your Faith. Don't take yourself so seriously that you lose sight of having fun with the family. Be sure to snap some photos too! Perhaps not now, but for sure later on, your family will love you for it!

FAMILY EVENING PRAYER
to be prayed each evening this week

Dear Lord, thank you for the blessings of this day—your day. If we have failed you in any way, please forgive us. If we have failed one another by not taking care of our responsibilities, please forgive us, Lord. Please help us to grow in holiness each day. We love you! Amen.

Pray: *Our Father, Hail Mary, Glory Be.*

Mary Leads Us to Jesus Sunday

"Mary embraces God's will and freely chooses to cooperate with God's grace, thereby fulfilling a crucial role in God's plan of salvation. Throughout the centuries, the Church has turned to the Blessed Virgin in order to come closer to Christ."
—United States Conference of Catholic Bishops[18]

FAMILY MORNING PRAYER

Read the verse above and pray the Morning Offering together as a family.

Morning Offering: Dear Lord Jesus, thank you for the gift of today— your Sunday. Please guide our family as we strive to grow closer to you and to one another. Open our hearts and teach us to be much more generous with our time. Open our eyes to discover opportunities to love others. Amen.

Pray: *Our Father, Hail Mary, Glory Be.*

REFLECT

The title of our reflection is: "Mary Leads Us to Jesus Sunday." Of course, we know that Mary *always* leads us to Jesus. But, on this Sunday, let us focus on that. Our Mother in heaven loves us so much and desires to continually lead us toward her Son so that we will enjoy our Eternal Life in heaven one day. The Church teaches that the Blessed Mother has always fully embraced her role in salvation history, united to her Son, Jesus. Through Mary's loving vocation, the faithful have been and will always be directed toward Jesus. The United States Conference of Catholic Bishops, from the source quoted at the head of this chapter, stated:

Mary embraces God's will and freely chooses to cooperate with God's grace, thereby fulfilling a crucial role in God's plan of salvation. Throughout the centuries, the Church has turned to the Blessed Virgin in order to come closer to Christ. Many forms of piety toward the Mother of God developed that help bring us closer to her Son. In these devotions to Mary, "while the Mother is honored, the Son, through whom all things have their being and in whom it has pleased the Father that all fullness should dwell, is rightly known, loved and glorified and . . . all His commands are observed." The Church honors her as the Mother of God, looks to her as a model of perfect discipleship, and asks for her prayers to God on our behalf.

Make today a "Mary day." Focus on her great love for you and your family and the fact that she spent her whole life cooperating with God's grace to help you to get to heaven. She is still doing it now.

CHOOSE AN ACTIVITY

Blessed Mother crafts: Gather a few arts and crafts materials: wooden clothespins with round tops, pieces of blue and white felt, embroidery floss for tying around the waist, pipe cleaners for Mary's arms, and craft glue. Have fun creating a Mother Mary and Baby Jesus figurine using these materials.

You will cut the felt to a size suitable to wrap around the clothespin to make Mother Mary. A separate smaller piece of felt can be used as a veil for the Blessed Mother. Baby Jesus can be made from a clothespin that has been cut or broken to "baby size." Then, swaddle it with felt to make the little Christ Child. Decorate as you and the children desire. Glue Baby Jesus against Mary as if she has him in her arms. The older children can assist the young ones. Have fun!

A simple drawing: To remember Mary's great love for her Son, Jesus, encourage the children to draw a picture of the Blessed Mother standing at the foot of Jesus on the Cross.

Paper doll Mary and Baby Jesus craft: Make simple "paper dolls" with construction paper, crayons or paints, tape or Velcro, and a craft stick or Popsicle stick. Simply draw and cut out a shape for Mary. Picture it like an upside-down letter "U." The bottom will be straight across, and that is where to attach a craft stick (to the back). Draw a simple oval face and hair for Mary, with a veil on her head. Make separate arms attached to hands that can come off the paper doll (with tape or Velcro on the backs). Make a separate piece that will be her Immaculate Heart. Also make a separate crown. If desired, make a small rosary piece that can be attached to Mary's hands. Have fun with it! As the children play with the paper dolls, teach them about Mary!

NOTE TO PARENTS AND GRANDPARENTS

Talk to the children about the need to have time for prayer and time for wholesome fun. They should spend time together, as well. If they are tempted to argue, they should instead pause and say a little prayer. Tell them that Mother Mary desires that they love one another.

MINI TEACHING

In an article for the *Our Sunday Visitor Newsweekly*, "What Catholics Need to Know about Making Their Homes a Domestic Church: How Parents Can Make Their Families 'Islands of Christian Life,'" I wrote about the role of parents in their domestic church and their teachings and guidance as a curriculum of love. I said:

> Catholic parents can look to the Catechism of the Catholic Church for direction regarding their responsibilities to impart the faith to their children. There we learn, "The Christian home is the place where children receive the first proclamation of the faith. For this reason the family home is rightly called 'the domestic church,' a community of grace and prayer, a school of human virtues and of Christian charity" (No. 1666).
>
> Within the walls of the domestic church, children learn about their faith through their parents' and grandparents' word and

example, as well as within the many growing pains and nitty-gritty details of everyday life as a family grows together in holiness.[19]

A lot happens—certainly much more than meets the eye in the midst of our ordinary days in the family. God has blessed us with one another. We are to help one another work out our salvation. That indeed happens during the give-and-take of our lives—through showing tenderness and love, as well as forgiveness—lots of forgiveness! Strive to be mindful of this. I will include more on this subject in our next chapter.

PONDER

Consider how you can be a more radiant example of Christ's love to your family. Have fun with your family today. Never take yourself too seriously. You are growing together.

FAMILY EVENING PRAYER
to be prayed each evening this week

Dear Lord, thank you for the blessings of this day—your day. If we have failed you in any way, please forgive us. If we have failed one another by not taking care of our responsibilities, please forgive us, Lord. Please help us to grow in holiness each day. We love you! Amen.

Pray: *Our Father, Hail Mary, Glory Be.*

Family Event Sundays

"The Christian home is the place where children receive the first proclamation of the faith. For this reason the family home is rightly called 'the domestic church,' a community of grace and prayer, a school of human virtues and of Christian charity."
—Catechism of the Catholic Church, no. 1666

T he endless blessings of a family can never truly be counted! Indeed, they are ongoing! Yet, throughout our busyness, we might neglect to thank God for his many blessings to us in the family. We should strive to be more thankful to God and to one another. We must learn to be quick to forgive our family members. We need to ask for their forgiveness. This is foundational to harmony within a Christian family. Make no mistake about it, with the exception of the Holy Family, every family is imperfect and must work hard to please God and help our family members.

This part of the book focuses on various family events that should be celebrated. Among them are these: sacraments, birthdays, anniversaries, graduations, family reunions, vacations, and new babies! You might already have your own unique reasons to celebrate that are not listed here. By all means, celebrate your family! Create your memories together, all the while trying your best to live within your present moments.

Sacrament or Birthday Sunday

"Christ instituted the sacraments of the new law. There are seven: Baptism, Confirmation (or Chrismation), the Eucharist, Penance, the Anointing of the Sick, Holy Orders and Matrimony. The seven sacraments touch all the stages and all the important moments of Christian life: they give birth and increase, healing and mission to the Christian's life of faith. There is thus a certain resemblance between the stages of natural life and the stages of the spiritual life."
—CCC, no. 1210

FAMILY MORNING PRAYER

Read the verse above and pray the Morning Offering together as a family.

Morning Offering: Dear Lord Jesus, thank you for the gift of today—your Sunday. Please guide our family as we strive to grow closer to you and to one another. Open our hearts and teach us to be much more generous with our time. Open our eyes to discover opportunities to love others. Amen.

Pray: *Our Father, Hail Mary, Glory Be.*

REFLECT

Sacrament certificates: Today is "Sacrament or Birthday Sunday." Are yours and your family's sacrament certificates stored away? A dear priest friend used to tell his congregation that our baptismal day could be considered even more important than our birthday. He knew that our birthday was important, of course. However, he emphasized that our Baptism initiates us into the Church! Father Bill encouraged everyone to frame and hang their certificates. Because of his teachings, my baptismal and First Holy Communion certificates are hanging on my bedroom walls. They remind me of who I am as a Catholic, but also, they remind me to celebrate those special days with great gusto! Whether you are celebrating a birthday or a sacrament, enjoy it all and take pictures. Try not to get overly elaborate in your planning and carrying out such a multitude of details that you can't even enjoy it. Don't make too much work for yourself. Find a happy balance.

CHOOSE AN ACTIVITY

Put your heads together to plan a celebration for a sacrament or birthday! Certainly, the day should not go by without a bit (or a lot!) of fun fanfare! Celebration is definitely in order and just might include a cake or special dessert. Perhaps a candlelight dinner will be on the agenda, or a trip out for an ice cream sundae! Celebrate with great gusto and make your memories!

NOTE TO PARENTS AND GRANDPARENTS

Special occasions such as birthdays and sacramental days deserve special treatment! The family is a unique and blessed place in which to share hearts and celebrate with one another. Family Sundays may not always be "picture perfect," so as much as you plan for a wondrous celebration, try not to be overly concerned about perfection. Talk to the children about the need to be more selfless and to strive to be more giving within the family, and in all circumstances. Let them know that their warm reaching out to their family members and others makes for happy experiences and can be transforming to someone who is feeling stressed or depressed.

MINI TEACHING

There's always so much to do in the family. Some would say it keeps us young! Others might say that it makes us feel old! Sometimes our to-do lists seem to be a mile long. Or, we have multiple lists—that would be me! Somehow, we survive. It's really all about God's grace and our desiring hearts. God wants us parents and grandparents to really make a holy difference in our family's life.

We compete with the bombardment from our contemporary culture, which does not usually mirror our godly values. Most times it does not. All the more reason for us to step up to the plate to teach and protect our family, crazy busy schedules and all. In the article that I mentioned in the last chapter, "What Catholics Need to Know about Making Their Homes a Domestic Church," I talk about some of the important happenings in the domestic church:

> Everyday life in the family may seem filled with a lot of ordinariness and at times a bit of chaos. Yet, right there along with the normal routines and day-to-day occurrences of sibling rivalry, teenaged angst and sometimes grouchy spouses is woven a paradigm of human enrichment pointing us to a narrow path that leads to heaven. Catholic teachings open our eyes to the remarkable goings on within a growing faithful Catholic family, helping us recognize that there is a heck of a lot more happening in our day-to-day lives than what meets the eye.
>
> "It is here that the father of the family, the mother, children, and all members of the family exercise the priesthood of the baptized in a privileged way 'by the reception of the sacraments, prayer and thanksgiving, the witness of a holy life, and self-denial and active charity.' Thus the home is the first school of Christian life and 'a school for human enrichment.' Here one learns endurance and the joy of work, fraternal love, generous—even repeated—forgiveness, and above all divine worship in prayer and the offering of one's life" (No. 1657).
>
> Amazing! And we thought we were simply teaching our kids how to share, love and pray, potty training them, breaking up fights, functioning as lovingly as possible after sleepless nights, laying down the law, and rescuing them from far too many lurking dangers. But in reality it is within the domestic church that Catholic parents lay out a curriculum of fraternal love and forgiveness while helping the family to work out their salvation in the give-and-take of life in the family.

PONDER

Consider the great love that God has for your family. Think about ways that you can lovingly ignite a huge spark of Faith in your family members' hearts. A big part of that is in being an exemplary Christian example to your family and others. Pray for the graces to more readily push a bit beyond your comfort zone to bring Christ's love to others—starting first with your family.

FAMILY EVENING PRAYER
to be prayed each evening this week

Dear Lord, thank you for the blessings of this day—your day. If we have failed you in any way, please forgive us. If we have failed one another by not taking care of our responsibilities, please forgive us, Lord. Please help us to grow in holiness each day. We love you! Amen.

Pray: *Our Father, Hail Mary, Glory Be.*

Anniversary or Graduation Sunday

"Clap your hands, all you peoples;
shout to God with loud songs of joy."
—Psalm 47:1

FAMILY MORNING PRAYER

Read the verse above and pray the Morning Offering together as a family.

Morning Offering: Dear Lord Jesus, thank you for the gift of today—
your Sunday. Please guide our family as we strive to grow closer to you
and to one another. Open our hearts and teach us to be much more
generous with our time. Open our eyes to discover opportunities to love
others. Amen.

Pray: *Our Father, Hail Mary, Glory Be.*

REFLECT

Today you will celebrate, or perhaps plan a celebration for, a wonderful
milestone in a family member's life. That could be a graduation or an
anniversary of some sort. Think about how you would like to celebrate.
Here are ideas to consider:

What type of setting will it be?

Is it a surprise for someone?

Does it involve doing something outside of your home?

Would you like to include celebratory and meaningful music?

Will there be dancing (hence the need of a "dance floor" of sorts)?

Will you invite anyone other than your family?

Might prayer be a part of this celebration?

Will a special recipe for a favorite dish be a part of this celebration?

CHOOSE AN ACTIVITY

"On This Day" reflection: Whether you will be celebrating an anniversary or a graduation today or soon, you can gather the family to sit at the family table for a time of reflection and prayer that will no doubt bring smiles. It's possible you will do this activity without the person of honor present. That way the end result will be a surprise to them. Provide colorful construction paper, crayons or pens, markers, and maybe some stickers too. After praying an Our Father together, ask each family member to take a few moments to reflect and then answer these questions (below) either in drawings or words. The younger ones can seek help from you or older siblings. Everyone can decorate their pages as desired.

1. What is the best thing about [the person you are celebrating]?

2. What is the funniest thing about him or her?

3. What did he or she do that made your heart happy?

4. What are your best words of advice for him or her?

Staple together to make a booklet out of the decorated pages of responses. Add a cover with the name of the person of honor. Present the booklet to the honored person at the celebration.

NOTE TO PARENTS AND GRANDPARENTS

As always, since it is the Lord's Day, you will want to be sure to participate at holy Mass either at the vigil Mass on Saturday night or today. Talk to the children about the need to worship together, spend time together, be good to one another.

MINI TEACHING

We read in Psalm 100:1–5, "Make a joyful noise to the LORD, all the earth. Worship the LORD with gladness; come into his presence with singing. Know that the LORD is God. It is he that made us, and we are his; we are his people, and the sheep of his pasture. Enter his gates with thanksgiving, and his courts with praise. Give thanks to him, bless his name. For the LORD is good; his steadfast love endures forever, and his faithfulness to all generations."

These are encouraging words—music to a believer's ears. They tell us that God made us and we are his. He is good and faithful. His steadfast love will endure forever. We are encouraged to worship God with gladness and praise him with "a joyful noise." Can we do that? Can we worship God with gladness? Even when we are weary? I believe that we can and that we should. Be sure to include our dear Lord in all of your family celebrations. Not only will you be praising God and pleasing him; you will be establishing an essential and firm foundation for your family.

PONDER

Consider how you might better "make a joyful noise to the Lord." It's essential to carve out the time for praising God. Sometimes we are weary or might be feeling a bit defeated—but all the more reason to smile and shout out with joy! God is here!

FAMILY EVENING PRAYER

to be prayed each evening this week

Dear Lord, thank you for the blessings of this day—your day. If we have failed you in any way, please forgive us. If we have failed one another by not taking care of our responsibilities, please forgive us, Lord. Please help us to grow in holiness each day. We love you! Amen.

Pray: *Our Father, Hail Mary, Glory Be.*

Family Reunion or Vacation Sunday

"Since parents have conferred life on their children, they have a most solemn obligation to educate their offspring. Hence, parents must be acknowledged as the first and foremost educators of their children. Their role as educators is so decisive that scarcely anything can compensate for their failure in it. For it devolves on parents to create a family atmosphere so animated with love and reverence for God and others that a well-rounded personal and social development will be fostered among children. Hence, the family is the first school of those social virtues which every society needs."

—Declaration on Christian Education, *Gravissimum Educationis*, no. 3

FAMILY MORNING PRAYER

Read the verse above and pray the Morning Offering together as a family.

Morning Offering: Dear Lord Jesus, thank you for the gift of today—your Sunday. Please guide our family as we strive to grow closer to you and to one another. Open our hearts and teach us to be much more generous with our time. Open our eyes to discover opportunities to love others. Amen.

Pray: *Our Father, Hail Mary, Glory Be.*

REFLECT

Today is a good day to plan a family vacation or "staycation." As well, you might also be planning a family reunion. Of course, you can even combine the celebrations. Life can get so busy that we don't make the efforts to plan celebrations. We might be too tired to even think about it! Or, we can't quite figure out how to schedule it. Planning far in advance is the key. As well, with regard to vacations, many things can get in the way of taking a vacation or even a "staycation" (when you can still do fun things but not go away). What are some considerations?

Family reunion: How many people will be invited? What time of year will this be? Will there be a set menu, catered, or potluck? If potluck, will you enlist help from others? Will there be music or dancing? Will it be at your home or at another location? Will you enlist help for decorating? Will there be a schedule—a set of events, or games? Will your children help with planning games?

Vacation: Will this be a vacation or staycation? How long will it be? When will it take place? Make a list of five desired destinations, or for a staycation, five local fun and inspiring places. For a vacation or a staycation, what holy sites can you incorporate? Do you need pet care? Now is a good time to look into costs and other details. Do you need to save money in order to plan your trip(s)? Figure out how much per week, and start putting it away.

CHOOSE AN ACTIVITY

I'd like to encourage you to plan your family reunion by letting you know about my friends Bob and Blanche, a couple from my parish. Bob comes from a family of fourteen boys and four girls! And Blanche's family has twelve children! Bob shared with me that his family plans a family reunion every year and has been doing so for forty-four years thus far! He said he's only missed two of them. I am inspired to carry out family reunions on a more regular basis after speaking with Bob.

NOTE TO PARENTS AND GRANDPARENTS

Talk to the children about the beautiful blessing of family, and give them a chance to list at least three ways that they are grateful for their family. Also, have them list ideas for a family reunion and family vacation or staycation.

MINI TEACHING

As parents, grandparents, and caregivers, we have an amazing and high calling as educators of the Faith for the children. Whether we live in a palace or a hut, Catholic parents have the awesome responsibility of raising their children not only to learn right from wrong, but to recognize that the real purpose of their lives in this world is to work out their salvation for the next world—their eternal lives. This has to be the number-one priority in raising Christian children. God provides the blessing of a family structure to accomplish this.

Today's verse teaches us, "Since parents have conferred life on their children, they have a most solemn obligation to educate their offspring. Hence, parents must be acknowledged as the first and foremost educators of their children. Their role as educators is so decisive that scarcely anything can compensate for their failure in it. For it devolves on parents to create a family atmosphere so animated with love and reverence for God and others that a well-rounded personal and social development will be fostered among children. Hence, the family is the first school of those social virtues which every society needs."

We also learn from that same document: "The role of parents in education is of such importance that it is almost impossible to provide an adequate substitute." God is counting on us! As well, the Catechism tells us, "Parents have the first responsibility for the education of their children. They bear witness to this responsibility first by creating a home where tenderness, forgiveness, respect, fidelity, and disinterested service are the rule. The home is well suited for education in the virtues. This requires an apprenticeship in self-denial, sound judgment and self-mastery—the preconditions of all true freedom. Parents should teach their children to subordinate the 'material and instinctual dimensions to interior and spiritual ones'" (CCC, no. 2223).

We must always bear in mind that because of our special responsibilities, parents will ultimately be answering to God with regard to how their children have been educated. It's up to us to investigate all that is going on in our children's education, not simply at home, but also in their schools, both Catholic and public, and their religious education programs.

PONDER

Can you carve out additional time for prayer—even a couple of minutes a few times a day? As you pray, try to be quiet, remembering that a conversation goes two ways. Allow God time to whisper to your heart and soul.

FAMILY EVENING PRAYER
to be prayed each evening this week

Dear Lord, thank you for the blessings of this day—your day. If we have failed you in any way, please forgive us. If we have failed one another by not taking care of our responsibilities, please forgive us, Lord. Please help us to grow in holiness each day. We love you! Amen.

Pray: *Our Father, Hail Mary, Glory Be.*

CHAPTER 36

Saint's Name Sunday

"The saints have always been the source and origin of renewal in the most difficult moments in the Church's history."
—Saint John Paul II, in Catechism of the Catholic Church, no. 828

FAMILY MORNING PRAYER

Read the verse above and pray the Morning Offering together as a family.

Morning Offering: Dear Lord Jesus, thank you for the gift of today—your Sunday. Please guide our family as we strive to grow closer to you and to one another. Open our hearts and teach us to be much more generous with our time. Open our eyes to discover opportunities to love others. Amen.

Pray: *Our Father, Hail Mary, Glory Be.*

REFLECT

Today we celebrate saints' name days! When your children and grand-children were baptized, they were ushered into the Church with at least one saint's name that was chosen specifically for them—perhaps by you! Throughout their lives you can call upon their patron saint for guidance and assistance for their journey through life. You can plan or carry out a special Saint's Name Day celebration for one or all of your children. Ponder how you would like to do it. The sky is the limit! Make today celebratory by lighting candles at the dinner table.

CHOOSE AN ACTIVITY

Saint's Name Day craft: Gather art supplies and talk to the children about their patron saints. You can tell them why you named them after a particular saint. This discussion can inspire their hearts to strive for sanctity. Research their saints online or in saints' books. Have the children focus on a couple of their saint's attributes or patronages, and ask them to illustrate the saint showing their qualities or charisms. Help them with this. Hang up their finished creations to admire.

Saint recipes: Research recipes that would relate to your child's patron saint. For instance, you might think of Irish soda bread for Saint Patrick since he was Irish. Or, you might discover a recipe that was common to the time when a particular saint lived. Have fun with this, and plan a meal or dessert around your findings. Perhaps you'll decide to make a special cake or cupcakes to celebrate the occasion.

Saint party: What was the world like at the time your saint was alive? Did he or she live in a castle, a monastery, or a convent, or a simple home? Create a special atmosphere in honor of your child's patron saint with music or decor that is reminiscent of the time of the saint. If possible, include a food dish from their era.

NOTE TO PARENTS AND GRANDPARENTS

Talk to the children about their patron saints. Remind your children that saints were just like us—a work in progress. However, they chose to pick themselves up, with God's help, if they fell into sin. They prayed for grace to continue to walk in Faith and worked out their salvation within the details of their lives. In addition, they will pray for us, for they want us to get to heaven too!

MINI TEACHING

The Church teaches that as baptized Catholics, we are part of the communion of saints. The Catechism states, "After confessing 'the holy catholic Church,' the Apostles' Creed adds 'the communion of saints.' In a certain sense this article is a further explanation of the preceding: 'What is the Church if not the assembly of all the saints?' The communion of saints is the Church" (CCC, no. 946). We can certainly feel blessed knowing that we are a member of the Church, as well as the communion of saints, which is joined together with the purpose of getting to heaven to live in complete happiness with God. We help one another reach that eternal goal.

There are three branches of the communion of saints. We are part of the Church Militant, which means we are living in the world and working out our salvation here within the nitty-gritty details of life. We are actually fighting a battle. We might not always be aware of it, though, because it is invisible. The evil one, who never sleeps, is constantly trying to trip us up. His earnest goal is to drag us to hell! Not a pleasant thought, but I cannot mince words. There's too much at stake. The Church Triumphant is the branch of the communion of saints in heaven who behold the Face of God. They pray for us, that we will make it to heaven, and they pray for the souls in purgatory as well. The Church Suffering consists of the holy souls in purgatory awaiting the heavenly banquet. They need our prayers, and they pray for us. They cannot pray for themselves.

The Church teaches, "Since all the faithful form one body, the good of each is communicated to the others. . . . We must therefore believe that there exists a communion of goods in the Church." And, we are reminded who it is that joins us together: "But the most important member is Christ, since he is the head. . . . Therefore, the riches of Christ are communicated to all the members, through the sacraments" (CCC, no. 947).

PONDER

You are truly a saint-in-the-making. As you pray, allow God to make you new so you will be an exemplary Christian example to your family and others. Don't forget to smile, laugh, and play. You will be creating beautiful experiences and memories for your family.

FAMILY EVENING PRAYER
to be prayed each evening this week

Dear Lord, thank you for the blessings of this day—your day. If we have failed you in any way, please forgive us. If we have failed one another by not taking care of our responsibilities, please forgive us, Lord. Please help us to grow in holiness each day. We love you! Amen.

Pray: *Our Father, Hail Mary, Glory Be.*

Holiday and Feast Sundays

"A saint was once asked, while playing happily with his companions, what he would do if any angel told him that in a quarter of an hour he would die and have to appear before the judgment seat of God. The saint properly replied that he would continue playing because I am certain these games are pleasing to God."
—Saint John Bosco[20]

Holidays and feast days are not only a lot of fun, but they are educational too. We should weave celebrations into the fabric of our lives. After all, there is so much to celebrate!

Each day gives us reason to celebrate. We have another day to give and receive love, to make things right, and to choose the high road and not snap back at someone who insults us or when we are faced with a choice of good or evil. Celebrations lift the spirit and unite people together. So, this part of *Reclaiming Sundays* consists of Sunday celebrations such as "Crafty Sunday," "Field Trip Sunday," "Sunday Brunch Sunday," and "Jesus Is Lord Sunday." If any attract your attention, then jump right in!

Will you bake a cake or make a dessert together? Will you light a candle, sing a song, or say a special prayer? Will you make a favorite comfort-food recipe or discover a new one? Ponder Saint John Bosco's words and make your Sundays full of joy! Take time to play and to celebrate, rejoice, and be glad!

CHAPTER 37

Crafty Sunday

"Be merry, really merry. The life of a true Christian should be a perpetual jubilee, a prelude to the festivals of eternity."
—Saint Theophane Vena [21]

FAMILY MORNING PRAYER

Read the verse above and pray the Morning Offering together as a family.

Morning Offering: Dear Lord Jesus, thank you for the gift of today—your Sunday. Please guide our family as we strive to grow closer to you and to one another. Open our hearts and teach us to be much more generous with our time. Open our eyes to discover opportunities to love others. Amen.

Pray: *Our Father, Hail Mary, Glory Be.*

REFLECT

Saint Theophane Vena emphasizes that our lives should be "merry"—and not simply "merry," but "really merry." I love that he underscores that essential trait of a true Christian. He says our lives should be a "perpetual jubilee" because they are a "prelude to the festivals of eternity." If only we could live our lives in that fashion and not allow the downers in life to cause us to sink. The truth is that we certainly can live joyfully. With God's help we can possess a deep and abiding joy in our hearts, knowing that there is a magnificent Eternal Life that follows our earthly lives. Mother Teresa often preached about the necessity of joy in our hearts. She even cautioned her Sisters that if they didn't possess God's joy in their hearts, they might as well pack up and go home. That is because the poor and needy do not deserve to have a grouchy person caring for them. This is something to think about.

CHOOSE AN ACTIVITY

Since today is "Crafty Sunday" perhaps you'll be enjoying making crafts. Even if you don't necessarily have a plan in mind, take the arts and crafts supplies out and gather around the kitchen or dining room table. In light of today's verse that begins our Sunday reflection, perhaps you can focus on the virtue of joy. Ask the children about joy in their hearts. Ask them to express how God's joy makes them feel. You too can make an illustration of joy! Read Luke 2:1–20 to the family when you sit down to make a craft. It will give them ideas. While making your crafts, you can discuss this reading and/or any parts of the Joyful Mysteries.

Make a Joyful Rosary booklet: The Joyful Mysteries of the Rosary are five stories about the birth and life of Jesus Christ in the Holy Family. Specifically, they are these:

1) The Annunciation

2) The Visitation

3) The Nativity

4) The Presentation of the Child Jesus in the Temple

5) The Finding of the Child Jesus in the Temple

Staple or clip pages together to make a booklet for each child. The older children can help the younger ones. Put the title of the decade of the Rosary, or the "Mystery," at the top of five pages. Help the children to illustrate what happens in each of the Mysteries. This might be an ongoing project. You don't have to finish today.

Joyful placemats: Create colorful placemats for your kitchen or dining room table that illustrate the Joyful Mysteries of the Rosary. You can purchase supplies at a craft store or cut fabric to the appropriate sizes and use fabric markers to decorate.

Family tree craft: Discuss ways to make a family tree suitable for framing or hanging. It can simply be a handmade picture of a tree on which you will add to the branches the names of the children and perhaps grandchildren. This can be done with a craft material of your choice, cut out in sizes and shapes of your choosing. This craft does not have to be done in any particular way. The whole point is to work on it together and have fun creating it! It might take several days to complete it, depending upon how elaborate you'd like to be. The family tree will emphasize the fact that you are all a family and can prayerfully model yourselves after the Holy Family.

NOTE TO PARENTS AND GRANDPARENTS

Talk to the children about worshiping God on his day today, as well as being cooperative. Encourage them to spend time with the family and to set aside time for resting their eyes and minds away from screens and technology.

MINI TEACHING

In his Apostolic Exhortation, the *Joy of the Gospel*, no. 1, Pope Francis wrote:

> The Joy of the Gospel fills the hearts and lives of all who encounter Jesus. Those who accept his offer of salvation are set free from sin, sorrow, inner emptiness and loneliness. With Christ joy is constantly born anew. In this Exhortation I wish to encourage the Christian faithful to embark upon a new chapter of evangelization marked by this joy, while pointing out new paths for the Church's journey in years to come.

At times, we may question how joy can possibly enter our hearts when there is so much sorrow and pain in the world. However, even in pain, we can have joy. Amazingly, even in death. Jesus Christ himself teaches us how. On Palm Sunday in 2013, Pope Francis stated in a homily: "Jesus on the Cross feels the whole weight of the evil, and with the force of God's love he conquers it, he defeats it with his resurrection. This is the good that Jesus does for us on the throne of the Cross. Christ's Cross embraced with love never leads to sadness, but to joy, to the joy of having been saved and of doing a little of what he did on the day of his death." Talk to the family about authentic joy and why it needs to reside in our hearts.

PONDER

As you pray, allow God to heal you of all life's hurts and to make you new so you will be an exemplary joyful Christian example to your family and others. Don't forget to smile! Yes, life is serious, but it's essential to make room for joy—for playing and laughing! All the while, you are creating joyful experiences and memories for your family.

FAMILY EVENING PRAYER

to be prayed each evening this week

Dear Lord, thank you for the blessings of this day—your day. If we have failed you in any way, please forgive us. If we have failed one another by not taking care of our responsibilities, please forgive us, Lord. Please help us to grow in holiness each day. We love you! Amen.

Pray: *Our Father, Hail Mary, Glory Be.*

CHAPTER 38

Field Trip Sunday

"Hate what the world seeks and seek what it avoids."
—Saint Ignatius of Loyola

FAMILY MORNING PRAYER

Read the verse above and pray the Morning Offering together as a family.

Morning Offering: Dear Lord Jesus, thank you for the gift of today—your Sunday. Please guide our family as we strive to grow closer to you and to one another. Open our hearts and teach us to be much more generous with our time. Open our eyes to discover opportunities to love others. Amen.

Pray: *Our Father, Hail Mary, Glory Be.*

REFLECT

Today is "Field Trip Sunday." Will your field trip today (or soon) be to the local library, a farm, a basilica, or a shrine? Will it be a sort of pilgrimage? Talk among yourselves to formulate ideas for fun and inspiring places to visit. In addition, because we know that not every classroom has four walls, no doubt your chosen destination will also be educational. The children don't need to know that little factoid—it can be our little secret! Once when our family visited Cape Cod, Massachusetts, we took a tour of the Cape Cod Potato Chip factory. It was a memorable outing where we met interesting people. Have fun getting out and about whatever you decide to do!

CHOOSE AN ACTIVITY

Getting there: It's up to you to decide upon your field trip today. Allow the family to weigh in on ideas. If it will be a long trip in your vehicle or transit, be sure to prepare ahead with a few travel games. You can also make them up along the way. The time will pass a bit faster when you are having fun! As well, the traveling time can be used wisely to pray the family Rosary too. Family trips can be a bit stressful, as well as great fun. However, if you can all work together and be sure to pray, it will no doubt become etched in your happy memories. As well, a lot of the fun is in getting there—the actual trip! Be sure to enjoy it.

NOTE TO PARENTS AND GRANDPARENTS

Talk to the children about the need to use their good manners, get along with their family members, and be helpful and prayerful. All of the above are essential ingredients in a recipe for a fun family trip.

MINI TEACHING

Pope Francis warned of the danger of getting caught up in the pursuit of frivolous pleasure and becoming deaf to God's voice. It's not difficult to fall into this situation due to our busyness and the bombardment of the culture. Specifically, he said:

> The great danger in today's world, pervaded as it is by consumerism, is the desolation and anguish born of a complacent yet covetous heart, the feverish pursuit of frivolous pleasures, and a blunted conscience. Whenever our interior life becomes caught up in its own interests and concerns, there is no longer room for others, no place for the poor. God's voice is no longer heard, the quiet joy of his love is no longer felt, and the desire to do good fades. This is a very real danger for believers too. Many fall prey to it, and end up resentful, angry and listless. That is no way to live a dignified and fulfilled life; it is not God's will for us, nor is it the life in the Spirit which has its source in the heart of the risen Christ. (*The Joy of the Gospel*, no. 2)

Ponder this great danger and do your best to work at ways in which you can encourage your family not to be "covetous" and in search of "frivolous pleasures." Make sure that you consistently create an atmosphere of prayer within your domestic church. As well, keep the teachings going. For instance, you can easily teach the Faith weekly right at your dinner table using my book, *Feeding Your Family's Soul: Dinner Table Spirituality*. Remember Venerable Archbishop Fulton Sheen's wise words, "Dead bodies float downstream; it takes live bodies to resist the current." Let's not be dead bodies!

PONDER

Consider ways in which you can become more alive in your Faith. This is a plus for you, your family, and everyone near you. Have fun with the family. Make room for playing and laughing to create meaningful experiences and memories.

FAMILY EVENING PRAYER
to be prayed each evening this week

Dear Lord, thank you for the blessings of this day—your day. If we have failed you in any way, please forgive us. If we have failed one another by not taking care of our responsibilities, please forgive us, Lord. Please help us to grow in holiness each day. We love you! Amen.

Pray: *Our Father, Hail Mary, Glory Be.*

CHAPTER 39

Sunday Brunch Sunday

"When you sit down to eat, pray. When you eat bread, do so
thanking Him for being so generous to you."
—Saint Basil the Great

FAMILY MORNING PRAYER

Read the verse above and pray the Morning Offering together as a family.

Morning Offering: Dear Lord Jesus, thank you for the gift of today—
your Sunday. Please guide our family as we strive to grow closer to you
and to one another. Open our hearts and teach us to be much more
generous with our time. Open our eyes to discover opportunities to love
others. Amen.

Pray: *Our Father, Hail Mary, Glory Be.*

REFLECT

Every Sunday gives us a reason to celebrate. This week is about "Sunday
Brunch"—a happy meal—usually celebratory in nature. In addition, it
also mixes the sweet with the savory—almost anything can go when it
comes to brunch. Today is a perfect Sunday to get your family involved
with making a celebratory meal that you will enjoy together. You can plan
it in advance to carry out today. Or, you can put your heads together to
plan a wonderful brunch to enjoy next Sunday. It's entirely up to you.

CHOOSE AN ACTIVITY

Perhaps you will cook together today. Don't forget to put thought into a Sunday brunch. You might decide to include the overnight French toast recipe below. Here are some tips for a happy and tasty brunch!

Keep your menu simple, but tasty and even fun. Make a couple of prepare-ahead foods like French toast (my recipe below), waffles, pancakes, or a large omelet cut into wedges. Keep these dishes warm in an oven at low heat. If you decide upon waffles or pancakes as the main course, create a fun custom-topping bar that might include slices of fresh bananas, shredded coconut, berries, chocolate or carob pieces, and maybe even whipped cream. As well, provide pure maple syrup or honey.

Another idea is to enjoy make-your-own breakfast burritos. Simply provide a stack of whole-wheat or brown-rice tortillas, a bowl of scrambled eggs made ahead, small pieces of turkey bacon, shredded fresh lettuce and spinach, fresh grape tomato, sliced-thin and finely chopped red onion (for the adults), feta or shredded cheddar cheese, and perhaps sour cream or plain yogurt. Help the children assemble and roll up delicious burritos.

For added nutrition and fun, make ahead fruit smoothies that you will serve in small glasses or paper cups. Depending upon the size of your family, you'll need two to three cups of 100% fruit juice of your choice, one quarter to a half cup of plain yogurt, a half cup to a cup of frozen strawberries, and a sliced fresh banana. If desired, add a tablespoon of almond butter. You can experiment with proportions for desired consistency and amount. Blend in an electric blender until thoroughly blended.

Set the table for fun: Place kraft or butcher paper on the table rather than a table cloth. Place Mason jars filled with new crayons and washable markers on the table. Or, purchase plain place mats from a craft store (or make your own). The children and adults can have fun decorating the tablecloth or placemats! I suspect that you'll have so much fun with brunch that you will want to do it on a regular basis and will discover new recipes to make together. I encourage you to write the recipes down and include them in a recipe box or book that you can create. I talk about this activity in "Appendix 1: Meaningful Family Activities."

A special recipe: I have a special recipe that I love to make, usually on Christmas Eve to be enjoyed on Christmas morning. It's perfect for any brunch or breakfast.

I learned this recipe in an unusual way, which I'll tell you about in a minute. I love it because all the preparation is done ahead of time. Then on Christmas morning (or whenever), you simply pop the pan into the oven about forty-five minutes before you'd like to serve it. I like to serve this delicious dish with fresh fruit, which can be washed and prepared on a dish and placed in the refrigerator in advance to save you the trouble on Christmas morning. I sometimes also serve fresh muffins along with it. You may substitute a whole-grain baguette in the recipe for added nutrition. You can even use a gluten-free baguette. On Christmas morning, after placing this pan into the preheated oven, simply set the timer and then go and open your presents! It's so *easy*. That's the idea—to keep it simple and enjoy your loved ones.

A meaningful encounter in the grocery store: Here's my special and true story. One day while at my local food market, I came upon an elderly woman (whose name I later learned was Ellen). She was walking around the produce aisle looking a bit lost. She sounded as if she was talking to herself. Actually, she was, as I found out as I approached her. I asked if she needed any help. She proceeded to tell me that she had been looking for fresh blueberries for a recipe. Since the fresh blueberries were a bit expensive on that late December day, just two days before Christmas, she decided to opt for frozen berries.

I decided to walk with Ellen to the frozen-food department on the other side of the store. Ellen and I chatted along the way, and my new friend told me all about this fabulous recipe that she had seen in a magazine, and about how it is assembled on Christmas Eve to enjoy on Christmas morning. I was sold on the idea instantly and grabbed a bag of frozen blueberries myself and tossed them into my shopping cart. Ellen and I gathered up the remaining items we both would need for the special dish. Before parting company that afternoon, we exchanged phone numbers with the intention to chat again at some point.

We did talk on the phone after Christmas; we compared notes about our delicious overnight Christmas French toast, and we made a date to get together. That was several years ago. Since then, we've been out for tea several times, watched a Christian movie together at the theater, and chatted about our faith and our families time and time again. I even brought Ellen a rosary from one of my visits to Rome. Though she is not Catholic, she loved it and began praying the Rosary. We are still friends to this day. And to think that we met in a grocery store! I marvel over God's ways. He arranges beautiful serendipitous encounters that can turn into meaningful friendships. I believe he wants us to be attentive to needs as they unfold around us. I'm so glad that even in my hurry that day, our Lord drew my attention to Ellen.

So, I hope you enjoy this. I can't help thinking of Ellen and Christmas every time I make it. I pray that God will place a special friend in your life too.

RECIPE

Overnight Christmas Blueberry-Pecan French Toast

Ingredients

nonstick spray
baguette, cut into 20 one-inch slices (I use 1½ to 2 baguettes)
6 to 8 eggs
3 cups milk
1 cup brown sugar (I use honey instead)
Vanilla extract to taste (1 or 2 tsp.)
nutmeg to taste (I use cinnamon as well)
1 cup pecans, toasted
2 cups blueberries, fresh or frozen

Directions

Coat a 9 x 13-inch baking pan with nonstick spray, and arrange baguette slices in a single layer in the dish. I usually "cheat" and make more than one layer.

In a large bowl, whisk together eggs, milk, three-fourths of the brown sugar (or honey), vanilla, and nutmeg. Pour the mixture evenly over the bread.

Cover and chill the mixture overnight. There will appear to be a lot of moisture when the mixture goes into the refrigerator, but most of it will soak into the bread throughout the night.

Just before baking, sprinkle the remaining quarter cup of brown sugar (or honey), the pecans, and the blueberries over the top.

Bake in a 350° F oven for about 45–60 minutes or until golden and bubbling. (Check it at 45 minutes and keep an eye on it for the remainder of the time.) It should be a light golden brown on top, and the egg mixture should be completely cooked.

Serve hot with pure maple syrup. For an added treat, heat the syrup with extra blueberries to make blueberry-flavored syrup. You can serve with fresh fruit on the side and breakfast sausage or bacon too.

NOTE TO PARENTS AND GRANDPARENTS

Talk to the children about the need to spend time together. This is important for the family every day, of course, but most of all on Sunday.

PONDER

How can you become more alive in your Faith and share it with your family? Try to be cognizant of living in the present moments of your day. All the while, you are creating special experiences and memories for your family. The children won't look back twenty years from now and express that their best memories were when watching television or playing video games. They will thank you for your time spent with them—for all of the wonderful memories that you have created together.

FAMILY EVENING PRAYER
to be prayed each evening this week

Dear Lord, thank you for the blessings of this day—your day. If we have failed you in any way, please forgive us. If we have failed one another by not taking care of our responsibilities, please forgive us, Lord. Please help us to grow in holiness each day. We love you! Amen.

Pray: *Our Father, Hail Mary, Glory Be.*

Jesus Is Lord Sunday

"Thomas answered him, 'My Lord and my God!'"
—John 20:28

FAMILY MORNING PRAYER

Read the verse above and pray the Morning Offering together as a family.

Morning Offering: Dear Lord Jesus, thank you for the gift of today—your Sunday. Please guide our family as we strive to grow closer to you and to one another. Open our hearts and teach us to be much more generous with our time. Open our eyes to discover opportunities to love others. Amen.

Pray: *Our Father, Hail Mary, Glory Be.*

REFLECT

After Jesus rose from the dead, he appeared to his disciples that evening as they were hiding away behind locked doors in fear of the Jews. They didn't know what would become of them. Jesus stood among them and said, "Peace be with you." He then showed them his pierced hands and his side. Scripture tells us, "Jesus said to them again, 'Peace be with you. As the Father has sent me, so I send you.' When he had said this, he breathed on them and said to them, 'Receive the Holy Spirit. If you forgive the sins of any, they are forgiven them; if you retain the sins of any, they are retained'" (John 20:19–23).

His disciple Thomas was not there at the time. So, when the other disciples told Thomas that they had seen the Lord, he expressed, "Unless

I see the mark of the nails in his hands, and put my finger in the mark of the nails and my hand in his side, I will not believe" (v. 25). That is why he has acquired the name "Doubting Thomas." A week later, Jesus came to them again. This time Thomas was among them. The Bible tells us, "Although the doors were shut, Jesus came and stood among them and said, 'Peace be with you.' Then he said to Thomas, 'Put your finger here and see my hands. Reach out your hand and put it in my side. Do not doubt but believe'" (vv. 26–27).

What did "Doubting Thomas" do? Thomas answered Jesus, "'My Lord and my God!' Jesus said to him, 'Have you believed because you have seen me? Blessed are those who have not seen and yet have come to believe'" (vv. 28–29). Imagine that conviction from Jesus himself! Jesus tells all of us, "Do not doubt but believe."

CHOOSE AN ACTIVITY

"Jesus is Lord" should be always on our hearts and minds. On this particular Sunday, we can celebrate it with even more fervor.

Christ the King crown craft: Make a crown fit for a king—not just any king, but Jesus, the King of Kings! Gather the children and arts and craft supplies consisting of foil, construction paper, paper plates, markers, crayons, paints. Use your imagination to create colorful decorative crowns. Encourage the children to write a list (with your help) of attributes of Jesus. The list might include words and titles such as these: mighty, humble, King, King of Kings, Lord of Hosts, Hosanna, etc. As well, on the crown, they can write a little note to Jesus.

NOTE TO PARENTS AND GRANDPARENTS

Talk to the children about the need to worship the Lord every day, not only on Sunday. Be sure to form healthy prayer habits with them. These habits, along with God's amazing grace, will carry them through their lifetime.

MINI TEACHING

It's important as a parent or grandparent to be mindful of the atmosphere we create in our domestic churches. Throughout *Reclaiming Sundays*, you've seen tips and teachings about your domestic church, and you'll find additional encouragement and tools in the Conclusion.

Make time for prayer: This is paramount in a Catholic family. Our Catechism tells us, "The Christian family is the first place for education in prayer" (CCC, no. 2694). We must endeavor to lay down a foundation of prayer in our domestic churches. It will undoubtedly be one of the most important things we will ever do as Christian parents and grandparents, aunts and uncles.

Simply put, "A family that prays together stays together." Mother Teresa was famous for saying this. She adopted it from Father Patrick Peyton. Additionally, we know that prayer should come from the depths of our sincere and contrite hearts. Our earnest prayers stretch up like incense to reach God. It is through the gift of Faith that we pray. The Holy Spirit teaches the faithful to pray in great hope. We learn from the Psalms, "I waited patiently for the Lord; he inclined to me and heard my cry" (Ps. 40:1). Love is at the very core of prayer. Therefore, we see that the theological virtues of faith, hope, and love are tightly meshed together in the mystery of prayer.

Tips for handing down the gift of prayer: We can start with our own example of praying in the company of our family, showing them that we can offer up prayers at any time, whether there is a particular need or just a desire to thank God for his many blessings. As well, we should establish specific times to pray together as a family, such as morning and evening prayers, a family Rosary (or a decade), and Grace before and after meals. I believe that a gentle approach to teaching prayer is preferred over a strict regimented one. We want to impress upon our children that prayer is a personal, loving conversation with God. And, by establishing family times for prayer, we are helping our family form what I like to call "prayer habits."

Show your love! Let's not shy away from outwardly showing our Christian love for our spouse, our children, our neighbors, and the world. We should impress upon our children that they are loved by God and have been blessed with gifts to serve others too. Following Mother Teresa's advice, we start all of this in the family. She often said, "Love begins at home."

Make a prayer place! Setting up a prayer table or prayer corner provides a tangible way for the family to focus on prayer. And all throughout the daily give-and-take within the family, dealing with inconveniences, differences, and occasional outbursts and discord, the family learns the valuable lesson of lovingly offering it all to God right within the nitty-gritty details of ordinary life, ultimately helping one another get to heaven.

PONDER

Ponder ways in which you can become more alive in your Faith, expressing it, and being more attentive to the needs in your domestic church. Make room for fun—playing and laughing! Your loving smiles speak volumes to your children!

FAMILY EVENING PRAYER

to be prayed each evening this week

Dear Lord, thank you for the blessings of this day—your day. If we have failed you in any way, please forgive us. If we have failed one another by not taking care of our responsibilities, please forgive us, Lord. Please help us to grow in holiness each day. We love you! Amen.

Pray: *Our Father, Hail Mary, Glory Be.*

PART ELEVEN

Saintly Sundays

"The saints have a special place in the Body of Christ, which includes both the living and the dead. Through Christ we on earth remain in communion both with the saints in heaven and with the dead who are still in Purgatory."

—United States Conference of Catholic Bishops[22]

G od tells us in Scripture, "You shall be holy, for I am holy" (1 Pet. 1:16). We are all called to live a life of holiness. We do this by following the Commandments, loving God and our neighbor. As well, we can learn so much from the saints who have gone before us. They struggled through life, much like us. However, they picked themselves up, dusted themselves off, and continued to walk in faith with God's help, always demonstrating heroic virtues. The saints were called to holiness and answered the call. We are called to that same sanctity.

The Church teaches about the influence of the saints in *Lumen Gentium* (CCC, no. 7):

In the lives of those who, sharing in our humanity, are however more perfectly transformed into the image of Christ, God vividly manifests His presence and His face to men. He speaks to us in them, and gives us a sign of His

Kingdom, to which we are strongly drawn, having so great a cloud of witnesses over us and such a witness to the truth of the Gospel.

Throughout this part of *Reclaiming Sundays* your family will learn more about the saints. Saint Padre Pio gives us succinct spiritual advice when he says, "Pray, hope, and don't worry." Let's be sure to do just that.

CHAPTER 41

Saint Elizabeth of Hungary Sunday

"The saints, the members of the Church who have arrived at perfect union with Christ, join their wills to the will of God in praying for those in the Church who are still on their pilgrimage of faith."

—United States Conference of Catholic Bishops[23]

FAMILY MORNING PRAYER

Read the verse above and pray the Morning Offering together as a family.

Morning Offering: Dear Lord Jesus, thank you for the gift of today—your Sunday. Please guide our family as we strive to grow closer to you and to one another. Open our hearts and teach us to be much more generous with our time. Open our eyes to discover opportunities to love others. Amen.

Pray: *Our Father, Hail Mary, Glory Be.*

REFLECT

We will learn more about a special saint in our Church—Saint Elizabeth of Hungary. In imitation of her, try your best to foster an atmosphere of giving today in your domestic church. If anyone begins to act a bit self-centered, quickly remind them that our Lord does not want that. He wants us to serve one another!

CHOOSE AN ACTIVITY

Baking cookies or bread: In the spirit of St. Elizabeth of Hungary, who fed the poor, consider making cookies or bread for your family to enjoy—and make a double batch to share them also with others (a shut-in, an elderly neighbor, a food kitchen, someone who needs cheering up).

Gifting a meal: Sometime this week, consider making a meal for someone who could use help—or who has too little. If you are not aware of where the needs are in your community, check with your parish office. I have always found that needs exist closer to us than we might think. There are often elderly neighbors nearby to me who welcome a healthy meal.

NOTE TO PARENTS AND GRANDPARENTS

Find time to sit down with the kids and read the story of St. Elizabeth of Hungary. See below. You might like to read it at the breakfast table to begin your day with inspiration.

MINI TEACHING

Read this aloud to the family or have an older child do so.
Afterward, encourage discussion about the story. Ask simple questions.

Saint Elizabeth of Hungary was born in a place called Bratislava in 1207. She was Princess Elizabeth, the daughter of King Andrew of Hungary. In those times, it was common to be betrothed or promised in marriage at a young age. Princess Elizabeth was betrothed to Prince Ludwig at age four and married him at age fourteen. In that time, it was not unusual to marry at this age. They had three children. Although Elizabeth was a princess, she chose to live and dress simply. Each day, she took bread to hundreds of the poorest around. They came to know her for her great love and came to her gate each day hoping for food.

One day when Elizabeth was taking food to the poor, her husband, Prince Ludwig, saw her and stopped her because he wanted to see what she was carrying under her mantle. The food she was taking to the hungry poor miraculously changed into roses. On another occasion, Elizabeth decided to take in a dying leper and took care of him at her home. She placed him in her own bed. Her husband, Prince Ludwig, was enraged when he found out about this. Planning to get the leper out of the bed, he grabbed the bed sheets and turned them back sharply to see the leper in his bed. However, suddenly he miraculously realized that he was witnessing the literal embodiment of Jesus in the leper. He saw Jesus! We can think about the words of Jesus: "Whatever you do for the least of these who are members of my family, you do unto me" (see Matt. 25:40).

After Elizabeth's husband died, Elizabeth became a Third Order Franciscan and dedicated her life totally to prayer and penance, and she continued to take care of the poor. In 1231, Saint Elizabeth died in extreme poverty at the age of twenty-four and was canonized in 1235, when the Church proclaimed her a saint. She became known as the patroness of Catholic charities and of the Secular Franciscan Order because she devoted her life to the poor, sick, and suffering, showing them great love.

EXTRA CREDIT!

Talk to the children about your family's responsibility as Christians to take care of the poor as far as they are able. While we might not allow a leper into our own beds, we are all called to help the poor and unfortunate. Ask the children to give examples about how your family might be able to help the poor. Ask them if there are any ways that they can simplify in their own lives. As well, think about how your family can strive to see Jesus in the poor and serve them with Christ's love.

1. What kind of person was Saint Elizabeth of Hungary?

2. How can you be like her? Encourage the children to list three ways.

3. Do you think Saint Elizabeth's works of mercy were pleasing to God? Can yours be?

PONDER

Throughout your Sunday, make room for playing and laughing. Have fun with your family today in some special ways. Honor today as the Lord's Day.

FAMILY EVENING PRAYER

to be prayed each evening this week

Dear Lord, thank you for the blessings of another Sunday together—your day. If we have failed to grow in our Catholic faith, please forgive us. If we have failed one another by putting ourselves before our family and others, please forgive us, Lord. Please teach us your ways each day so that we can become more and more like you. Amen.

Pray: *Our Father, Hail Mary, Glory Be.* Saint Elizabeth of Hungary, please pray for us. Amen.

CHAPTER 42

Saint Zélie and Saint Louis Martin Sunday

"For every genuine testimony of love shown by us to those in heaven, by its very nature tends toward and terminates in Christ who is the 'crown of all saints,' and through Him, in God Who is wonderful in his saints and is magnified in them."

—*Lumen Gentium*, no. 7

FAMILY MORNING PRAYER

Read the verse above and pray the Morning Offering together as a family.

Morning Offering: Dear Lord Jesus, thank you for the gift of today—your Sunday. Please guide our family as we strive to grow closer to you and to one another. Open our hearts and teach us to be much more generous with our time. Open our eyes to discover opportunities to love others. Amen.

Pray: *Our Father, Hail Mary, Glory Be.*

REFLECT

During his homily on the canonization day of Saints Louis and Zélie Martin, Pope Francis pointed out the blessings that we can receive from the saints in heaven who can powerfully pray for all of us on earth—we who are desperately trying to get there one day. He stated, "The radiant witness of these new saints inspires us to persevere in joyful service to our brothers and sisters, trusting in the help of God and the maternal protection of Mary. From heaven may they now watch over us and sustain us by their powerful intercession."

Learn more about these saints below in our "Mini Teaching." Ponder the fact that through their steadfast love and teachings, Louis and Zélie Martin gave all of their children a sturdy foundation of Faith. Throughout the details of their lives, saints were made! This does not mean that it was effortless or Instagram picture perfect. It took work and perseverance. What about your domestic church? Can these parent saints inspire you?

CHOOSE AN ACTIVITY

Make a saint book: Gather the children and arts and craft supplies. Encourage each family member to create a saint book. Allow them to tell the story simply or elaborately in pictures and/or words. Put the date on the book. Staple or clip pages together. Place it on your prayer table or prayer corner to be enjoyed at any time.

NOTE TO PARENTS AND GRANDPARENTS

Talk to the children about the holiness of Sundays. Encourage them to seek God in a special way today. Invite them to ask Saints Zélie and Louis Martin to carry their prayer petition to God today.

MINI TEACHING

Saint Zélie and St. Louis Martin were the Roman Catholic parents of nine children. One is St. Therese of Lisieux, known as the Saint of the Little Way, and the Little Flower. Hailing from France, they are the first married couple to be canonized saints. Both were hard workers; Louis Martin was a watchmaker by trade and Zélie was a lace maker. Before meeting, they both had prayed to discern a religious vocation. But it was not meant to be. Instead, they met one another in Alençon, France, and decided to become married (1858). Zélie eventually bore nine children: seven girls and two boys. Sadly, two daughters and the two sons died young. The parents were sorrowful, but trusted God. They lovingly raised the remaining five girls, all of whom would eventually enter religious life! Saint Therese of Lisieux would say, "God gave me a father and a mother who were more worthy of heaven than of earth." She was canonized in 1925.

Zélie died of breast cancer at age forty-five. Soon after, all five daughters left for the religious life. Though lonely, and no doubt still sorrowful for the loss of his other children, Louis said, "It is a great, great honor for me that the Good Lord desires to take all of my children. If I had anything better, I would not hesitate to offer it to him." The Martins were beatified on October 19, 2008. On October 18, 2015, Pope Francis presided at a Mass in St. Peter's Square that included the Rite of Canonization for Saints Zélie and Louis Martin. Pope Francis stated in his homily, "The holy spouses Louis Martin and Marie-Azelie Guerin practiced Christian service in the family, creating day by day an environment of faith and love which nurtured the vocations of their daughters, among whom was St. Therese of the Child Jesus." He added, "They are the first-ever married couple with children to be canonized in the same ceremony." I feel very blessed to have visited and venerated the relics of Saints Louis and Zélie Martin in Lisieux, France.

PONDER

What are some ways you could become more alive in your Faith? Make time for God. Have fun with the family today. All the while, be assured that you are creating meaningful experiences and memories for your family.

FAMILY EVENING PRAYER

to be prayed each evening this week

Dear Lord, thank you for the blessings of this day—your day. If we have failed you in any way, please forgive us. If we have failed one another by not taking care of our responsibilities, please forgive us, Lord. Please help us to grow in holiness each day. We love you! Saint Louis and Saint Zélie, please pray for us! Amen.

Pray: *Our Father, Hail Mary, Glory Be.*

CHAPTER 43

Saint Bernadette Sunday

"When we look at the lives of those who have faithfully followed Christ, we are inspired with a new reason for seeking the City that is to come (274) and at the same time we are shown a most safe path by which among the vicissitudes of this world, in keeping with the state in life and condition proper to each of us, we will be able to arrive at perfect union with Christ, that is, perfect holiness."

—*Lumen Gentium,* no. 7

FAMILY MORNING PRAYER

Read the verse above and pray the Morning Offering together as a family.

Morning Offering: Dear Lord Jesus, thank you for the gift of today—your Sunday. Please guide our family as we strive to grow closer to you and to one another. Open our hearts and teach us to be much more generous with our time. Open our eyes to discover opportunities to love others. Amen.

Pray: *Our Father, Hail Mary, Glory Be.*

REFLECT

Today is a Sunday to learn about St. Bernadette and Our Lady of Lourdes. I was blessed to lead a pilgrimage to the Lourdes grotto and to see and venerate St. Bernadette's incorrupt body. Lourdes is an unforgettable holy place. In our "Mini Teaching" below, you will learn more about Our Lady of Lourdes and St. Bernadette. The exemplary example of the saints can be a wonderful aid to our spiritual journeys. Take time to ponder your role in the communion of saints. Do you strive to become a saint one day? That means working at it each day, choosing to practice the virtues and not allow the gravity of the ungodly world to pull you down. Do you pray for the holy souls in purgatory? Do you ask the saints to pray for you and your family?

CHOOSE AN ACTIVITY

Hopefully, you will read today's teaching below about St. Bernadette to your family. Ask them to share their thoughts afterwards. As well, ask them to list five ways that they can strive to be like her. Help them with this.

Our Lady of Lourdes craft: Do some research to find images of Our Lady of Lourdes and St. Bernadette. Gather the kids and the art supplies and draw pictures of the famous grotto. If you are ambitious, perhaps you will create a figurine of Mary and St. Bernadette out of clay or craft supplies. Ask your parish priest to bless it and place it on a prayer table in your home. As well, you can go online (https://www.lourdes-france.org/en/) if you'd like to learn more about the Sanctuary of Lourdes, see videos (sometimes live), and learn about the new St. Bernadette reliquary and more.

NOTE TO PARENTS AND GRANDPARENTS

Talk to the children about trying hard to live a life of holiness and not listen to the demands from the culture. Explain the differences between your domestic church and what is out in the world. Assure them of continual nourishment for their bodies *and* their souls. However, they need to open their hearts to it and to pay attention. God wants them to become saints!

MINI TEACHING

Saint Bernadette Soubirous was the first saint I learned about as a youngster. She was born in Lourdes, France, on January 7, 1844, the first child of François and Louise Soubirous. Her father was a good man and a miller by trade, but had a lot of trouble keeping work. Eventually, the mill that he ran that had belonged to his wife's family had to be forfeited due to debt. At times he escaped into alcohol, to the detriment of his wife and children. Louise was an exemplary Catholic and hard worker. She bore many children, only five of whom survived infancy.

As the oldest, Bernadette had many responsibilities in helping with the caring of the smaller children and household and farm chores. She had ill health and suffered from respiratory ailments from a young age. The family moved from one bad dwelling to another and ended up in a dark and damp place that had once served as a jail.

On February 11, 1858, when out with two other girls to fetch firewood, fourteen-year-old Bernadette saw a vision of the Blessed Mother. At the time, she did not know it was the Blessed Mother. However, in a further apparition on March 25, the Lady identified herself as the "Immaculate Conception." What Bernadette saw that day by the stream was a beautiful, luminous young Lady up in a niche of a rock. In that area of Lourdes, escarpments of rock were a common sight, the most famous being the Massabeille, which jutted out from the base of a plateau. Later, this place would become amazingly famous after the wondrous visits from the Queen of Heaven.

But, for now, let's get back to what Bernadette experienced on that cold February day. Bernadette was right by a stream, in the process of taking her stockings off so that she could cross the icy water and catch up with her sister and neighbor who had gone ahead of her. She had taken her time, not quite sure at first if she should wade through the icy water. It could throw her into an asthmatic fit or worsen her health.

Stockings in hand, suddenly, hearing a rustling of wind, Bernadette looked up toward the grotto and was amazed to see a radiant Lady dressed in white with a blue sash around her waist. Roses of a golden color adorned the Lady's feet. The Lady looked down and smiled at Bernadette. The young Soubirous child's initial fears immediately evaporated upon seeing the beautiful, warm smile. Bernadette instinctively began to pray the Rosary, and the Lady prayed silently as her own Rosary beads glided through her fingers. At the end of each decade the Lady prayed the Gloria with Bernadette.

This was the first of the many apparitions of Our Lady of Lourdes. On February 18, during the Lady's third visit to the niche of the rock, the Lady asked Bernadette to come there every day for fifteen days. Bernadette agreed to go to see the Lady as long as her parents would allow it. Bernadette would see the Lady on the remainder of visits, and the Lady instructed, "You will pray to God for sinners." On another visit, on February 26, at the Lady's bidding, Bernadette uncovered with her hands a hidden trickle of water. The young girl straightaway drank and bathed her face with the water. This trickle of water soon welled up to a steady flow that has not stopped flowing since that day in 1858. I was blessed to have seen it flowing at the famous Shrine that is there now in Lourdes, France. Our Lady of Lourdes had asked that a chapel be built on that sight.

Many townspeople and others went to visit the grotto. They wanted to be near the Lady if she should appear, and also near to Bernadette. However, as word started circulating throughout their small hamlet, Bernadette eventually suffered much due to scoffing, harassment, and disbelief. Authorities continually interrogated the young teen and tried to discredit her. The whole situation became stressful for her family as well. The poverty-stricken parents were accused of conjuring up a scheme to make money. The truth is that they did not accept any money or gifts that the townspeople offered. Eventually, Bernadette left home for the convent, which was filled with further challenges amid the holy joys, and where she in time took the veil. In September 1878, Bernadette made her perpetual and final vows as a nun.

There's much more to the story, but I have shared enough to hopefully sharpen your interest. I encourage you and your family to do your own research on St. Bernadette and many other saints who will certainly aid you on your journey toward heaven. Take time to discuss this story with your family after you have read it to them. Hopefully, you will have a very meaningful conversation. Carry it throughout the week. Perhaps you can do this by asking them what St. Bernadette would do in a particular situation that you might encounter during the week. Our Lady of Lourdes, please pray for us! Saint Bernadette, please pray for us!

PONDER

Think about young Bernadette and the fact that God used a simple peasant girl to deliver a heavenly message to the world. She listened, obeyed, and moved forward in Faith even when she was mocked by unbelievers. Make plenty of room for playing and laughing today and every day! All the while, you are creating marvelous experiences and memories for your family.

FAMILY EVENING PRAYER

to be prayed each evening this week

Dear Lord, thank you for the blessings of this day—your day. If we have failed you in any way, please forgive us. If we have failed one another by not taking care of our responsibilities, please forgive us, Lord. Please help us to grow in holiness each day. We love you! Our Lady of Lourdes, please pray for us! Saint Bernadette, please pray for us! Amen.

Pray: *Our Father, Hail Mary, Glory Be.*

CHAPTER 44

Saint Faustina Sunday

"It is supremely fitting, therefore, that we love those friends and coheirs of Jesus Christ, who are also our brothers and extraordinary benefactors, that we render due thanks to God for them and "suppliantly invoke them and have recourse to their prayers, their power and help in obtaining benefits from God through His Son, Jesus Christ, who is our Redeemer and Saviour."

—*Lumen Gentium*, no. 7

FAMILY MORNING PRAYER

Read the verse above and pray the Morning Offering together as a family.

Morning Offering: Dear Lord Jesus, thank you for the gift of today—your Sunday. Please guide our family as we strive to grow closer to you and to one another. Open our hearts and teach us to be much more generous with our time. Open our eyes to discover opportunities to love others. Amen.

Pray: *Our Father, Hail Mary, Glory Be.*

REFLECT

Today is all about St. Faustina. She grew up in a loving family in Poland, but they were poverty-stricken. In fact, the girls had to take turns going to Sunday Mass since there was only one church dress to be shared. Their father could not earn enough to provide for his family as he would have liked. But perhaps his robust example of prayer made up for it. You will learn much more in the teaching below.

CHOOSE AN ACTIVITY

Works of mercy: Since St. Faustina learned from Jesus about showing mercy to others, take time to plan family works of mercy that you can offer others. Jesus told St. Faustina to show mercy to others in three ways: by deed, word, and prayer. There are many opportunities that present themselves even in the course of one day. Parents and grandparents should discuss with the children the need to show mercy. We must seize the opportunities and not put them off. As well as being attentive to the needs that unfold around us, we must also strive to show mercy in other areas too.

NOTE TO PARENTS AND GRANDPARENTS

Talk to the children today about the need to show mercy to others, be together as a family, learn more about their Catholic Faith, be good to one another, and get rest and refreshment today on the Lord's Day!

MINI TEACHING

Read and explain to the children in a way they will understand.

Saint Faustina was born into a simple Polish peasant family on August 25, 1905. The third daughter of Stanislaus and Marianna Kowalska, she was baptized as Helen just two days later at St. Casimir Christ in Swine Warkie. The family lived in a simple house built by Stanislaus—limestone and red brick with a typical thatched roof.

The family struggled financially. With a war going on and many mouths to feed, Stanislaus tried his best to put food on the table. Times were restless in Poland. Russian teachers were steadily replacing Polish ones in the schools, and Russian had become the official language in the government and schools. There were plenty of bloody clashes as factory workers protested for better conditions and against autocratic rule.

Marianna was a hard worker, too, attentively raising the family, and was a fine baker of delicious breads that she churned out each day, despite having never read a recipe because of her illiteracy. Both she and her husband took seriously their role in teaching the Faith to their children. Marianna said, "The Faith was very important to [Stanislaus], which is what I liked about him. Though I could not read or write, I taught my daughters and sons the truths of the Gospel, taking care that they not only knew the precept of love of neighbor, but primarily, that they observed it."[24]

Helen was an obedient child and a favorite to her parents because of her obedience, her eagerness to help, and her docile disposition. At just seven years old, Helen had her first profound mystical experience when praying before the Blessed Sacrament at a Vespers service at her own parish church. Later on, when she was a teenager, she also had an amazing mystical experience. As well, she was regularly awakened at night by her Guardian Angel with flashes of light summoning her to prayer.

As Helen matured, she felt a distinctive calling to the religious life, but her father would not allow it. Though he was very spiritually minded, the family lacked the money for the dowry that would be required. Helen asked again, but received another refusal. Eventually, in time, Helen entered the convent. That was after a visit from Jesus himself. He appeared to her while she was at a dance and asked her straight out, "How long shall I put up with you and how long will you keep putting Me off?" He was rescuing her from a distracted and somewhat worldly life.

Helen was on a train headed for Warsaw the following morning. There, she would search for a convent that would open its door to her. It was quite a process, but a convent door finally opened, and she joined the Congregation of the Sisters of Mercy. Helen's name would now be Sister Maria Faustina Kowalska. Jesus again visited Sister Faustina. This time it was to entrust her with a huge mission. She was to become God's "Secretary of Divine Mercy" to promote the message of Divine Mercy to the world. This was not a new message of the Church, but it was presented in a new way. As with any important mission, many challenges and struggles ensued. Just because Sister Faustina lived in a convent didn't mean that her life was easy. It was quite the opposite. With God's grace though, she persevered.

Divine Mercy is a popular devotion in the Catholic Church. The image of Divine Mercy is central to the message. It shows Jesus with two rays coming forth from his heart. Jesus asked Sister Faustina to have this image painted when he visited her on February 22, 1931, to entrust her with so great a mission. Jesus said: "Paint an image according to the pattern you see, with the signature: Jesus, I trust in You. I desire that this image be venerated, first in your chapel, and [then] throughout the world. I promise that the soul that will venerate this image will not perish. I promise victory over [its] enemies already here on earth, especially at the hour of death. I Myself will defend it as My own glory."[25]

Later, Jesus explained to St. Faustina the meaning of the two rays in the image: "The two rays denote Blood and Water. The pale ray stands for Water which makes souls righteous. The red ray stands for Blood which is the life of souls. These two rays issued forth from the very depths of My tender mercy when My agonized Heart was opened by the lance on the Cross. These rays shield souls from the wrath of My Father. Happy is the one who will dwell in their shelter, for the just hand of God shall not lay hold of him. I desire that the first Sunday after Easter be the Feast of Mercy."[26]

Saint Faustina worked tirelessly to carry out her mission. She gave us reassuring words that she is not finished and will continue her work from heaven. I recommend that you read the *Diary* of Saint Faustina. Hers is a fascinating story. We can learn much from the humble soul.

PONDER

Do you know where our "good intentions" can lead us? On a road to hell. I'm sorry to be blunt, but I remember well as a young lady when I was once explaining my "good intentions" to someone, she quickly pointed out that "good intentions" only lead to hell. Yikes! They lead there, that is, if they are not carried out. Then, it is only an *intention* to do good. We have to act upon our Faith with good works. Good intentions are never enough. Saint James was very clear that Faith without works is dead. Specifically, he said, "For just as the body without the spirit is dead, so faith without works is also dead" (James 2:26). Let's not miss the opportunities to please God and serve our neighbor.

FAMILY EVENING PRAYER
to be prayed each evening this week

Dear Lord, thank you for the blessings of this day—your day. If we have failed you in any way, please forgive us. If we have failed one another by not taking care of our responsibilities, please forgive us, Lord. Please help us to grow in holiness each day and to be more merciful with others. We love you! Saint Faustina, please pray for us! Amen.

Pray: *Our Father, Hail Mary, Glory Be.*

PART TWELVE

Ordinary Time Sundays

"For the love of Christ urges us on."
—2 Corinthians 5:14

This part of *Reclaiming Sundays* is about Ordinary Time, a part of our Catholic liturgical year. Ordinary does not have to be so ordinary. I believe that it can be quite extraordinary. Strive to live within all of the present moments of your lives within your domestic church. Don't worry about the past. Give that to God. Don't worry about the future. Live right here—right now.

The United States Conference of Catholic Bishops tells us, "Ordinary Time is a time for growth and maturation, a time in which the mystery of Christ is called to penetrate ever more deeply into history until all things are finally caught up in Christ. The goal, toward which all of history is directed, is represented by the final Sunday in Ordinary Time, the Solemnity of Our Lord Jesus Christ, King of the Universe."[27]

Within this part of the book, you'll be able to choose from chapters such as Educational Sunday, Family Fun Sunday, Relative Sunday, and Discovery Sunday.

Educational Sunday

"Do not love the world or the things in the world. The love of the Father is not in those who love the world; for all that is in the world—the desire of the flesh, the desire of the eyes, the pride in riches—comes not from the Father but from the world. And the world and its desire are passing away, but those who do the will of God live forever."

—1 John 2:15–17

FAMILY MORNING PRAYER

Read the verse above and pray the Morning Offering together as a family.

Morning Offering: Dear Lord Jesus, thank you for the gift of today—your Sunday. Please guide our family as we strive to grow closer to you and to one another. Open our hearts and teach us to be much more generous with our time. Open our eyes to discover opportunities to love others today. Amen.

Pray: *Our Father, Hail Mary, Glory Be.*

REFLECT

Today's theme is education. We can make education fun while it nourishes our minds, hearts, and souls. Think about that and how our lives can be filled with learning. We should never stop learning until we draw our last breath. There is always something more. Continue to instill a love of learning in your little ones of all ages.

CHOOSE AN ACTIVITY

Since today is "Educational Sunday," what ways can you learn today while having fun? Might it be a trip to a historical museum or a science museum? If not today, then soon? Will you stay home and choose a subject to learn that all of you are interested in? Write down five choices after getting suggestions from the family. Put them in a hat or container and have someone draw one out. Devise a couple of creative ways to learn about your subject.

Educational board game: Get together with craft supplies and design a simple educational board game. It's not as complicated as you might think. After creating it, you will surely have fun playing it again and again!

Catechism activity. Open the Catechism to a teaching you would like to read to the family. Read it ahead of time to familiarize yourself with the material, and read it to the family tonight at the dinner table. It might just be one simple but powerful paragraph. Ask a few questions about the material to encourage a discussion. Try to do this often. You will learn right along with the family because there is a wealth of information contained in the Catholic Catechism!

Meditate while at rest: Encourage the family to use Sunday rest time to contemplate something holy. You can read a line or two from Scripture or from the lives of the saints and ask the family to take a few minutes to contemplate the truth as they rest.

NOTE TO PARENTS AND GRANDPARENTS

We can sometimes take our family for granted. However, being part of a family is being a part of a very special Catholic community! It is within the family setting that family members may openly share their hearts, trust one another, and grow in their Faith. Talk to the children about the need to appreciate their family, to share freely from their hearts, to help one another, to trust one another, to learn their Faith, and be cooperative learners!

MINI TEACHING

Christian life is countercultural to the way of the world. The scriptural quote that begins our Sunday reflection reminds us that the things of the world are not of God. Of course, there are many good things about the world. After all, God created it! However, I am referring to the ungodly things. To be a Christian means that we go against the flow of the world. As I quoted Archbishop Fulton Sheen in a previous reflection, "Dead bodies float downstream; it takes live bodies to resist the current." It's not easy to move out of our comfort zones to attempt to evangelize in our world today. Or, even to live in a countercultural way. Our children and grandchildren need our protection from the "lust" of the culture. We must impress upon them that the lies, sins, and distractions of the culture will make us sink, but "the will of God abides for ever."

On November 30, 2013, speaking to youth, Pope Francis delivered a powerful homily in which he emphasized the importance of staying true to the Faith in the face of modern ideals. He said, "If you don't let yourselves be conditioned by prevailing opinions, but remain faithful to Christian ethical and religious principles, you will find the courage even to go against the current." He lovingly cautioned, "The fullness of the Christian life that God carries out in man, in fact, is always threatened by the temptation to succumb to the spirit of the world. For this reason God gives us his aid by which we can preserve the gifts of the Holy Spirit, the new life in the Spirit that He has given us." He encouraged and reminded the youth that they need to call upon the Holy Spirit and the graces of their Baptism. "Dear young university students, your willpower and your capabilities, united to the power of the Holy Spirit that lives in each one of you from the day of your baptism, permits you to be not spectators, but protagonists in contemporary events."

He extolled them to step up to the plate and not become complacent. He said, "One can't live without looking at the challenges, without responding to the challenges." He reminded them, "God is more powerful than our weaknesses," adding that, "God's faithfulness never disappoints." Bearing in mind the pontiff's message to the youth, how can you encourage your own children and grandchildren to stand firm in Faith and not buckle under the demands and temptations of the culture that will lead them away from God? As well, how can they be a shining example of the truth of God's love to others? You can help them!

PONDER

What are some ways in which you can become more alive in your Faith, less complacent, and less conditioned by prevailing opinions? How can you help the children to do so as well? Your steadfast efforts will bear fruit in your children and grandchildren. Work hard and trust God, all the while loving them to heaven!

FAMILY EVENING PRAYER
to be prayed each evening this week

Dear Lord, thank you for the blessings of this day—your day. If we have failed you in any way, please forgive us. If we have failed one another by not taking care of our responsibilities, please forgive us, Lord. Please help us to grow in holiness each day. We love you! Amen.

Pray: *Our Father, Hail Mary, Glory Be.*

Family Fun Sunday

"The institution of Sunday helps all 'to be allowed sufficient rest and leisure to cultivate their familial, cultural, social, and religious lives.'"

—Catechism of the Catholic Church, no. 2194

FAMILY MORNING PRAYER

Read the verse above and pray the Morning Offering together as a family.

Morning Offering: Dear Lord Jesus, thank you for the gift of today—your Sunday. Please guide our family as we strive to grow closer to you and to one another. Open our hearts and teach us to be much more generous with our time. Open our eyes to discover opportunities to love others. Amen.

Pray: *Our Father, Hail Mary, Glory Be.*

REFLECT

The words in our verse today give us *permission* to have "sufficient rest and leisure to cultivate" our "familial, cultural, social, and religious lives." Don't hesitate to be sure that your family enjoys sufficient leisure as well as lots of family fun. Perhaps you can focus in a more vibrant way—a more cognizant way. Life is too short not to have lots of wholesome family fun. Put your heads together to come up with activities that will be most enjoyable and also doable today. Whatever you end up doing, be sure to have fun!

CHOOSE AN ACTIVITY

Focus on family fun today. One thing is for sure: if you are worried about tomorrow's "to-do list," you cannot focus on your family fun today. If your mind starts to go there—bring it back to this present moment.

Give thanks: Is this really an activity? Yes. And it is a teaching. Teaching the children to be appreciative requires effort and perseverance. Living in a fast-paced technological world of instant gratification sometimes means that today's children could tend to expect too much. Their friends might have all the latest gadgets, and your children and grandchildren question why they cannot have the same things. Take time to explain your Christian values, which don't include inordinate desires for too many material things. Also, be sure to fit in big doses of thanks to God and to one another. When we are thankful we become more positive. Our hearts are opened in a greater awareness of God's bountiful blessings, which can lead us to desire spiritual treasures, and in our responsibility to help others.

Angel mobile craft: Gather everyone together, as well as arts and crafts supplies. Have each family member draw a simple outline of an angel. Cut them out and decorate them. You can use a sparkly pipe cleaner formed in a circle for the halo. By tracing around the children's hands on colorful construction paper, and cutting them out, you will have wings to affix to the back of the paper figure. If desired, glue a photo of each person on their angel and attach a string or piece of yarn, and assemble them to form a mobile to hang in your kitchen or family area. If not a photo, print the prayer below, make copies, and glue one on to each angel. Your finished creation can remind everyone of their mighty Guardian Angel who protects them.

Angel of God Prayer

Angel of God, my guardian dear,
To whom God's love commits me here,
Ever this day, be at my side,
To light and guard, rule and guide.
Amen.

NOTE TO PARENTS AND GRANDPARENTS

Talk to the children about their Guardian Angel. Impress upon them that they should strive to be more grateful for all of the blessings in their lives and try not to be greedy for many material things. Encourage them to work together, pray together, have fun together, learn about their Faith, help others, and get rest on the Lord's Day.

MINI TEACHING

Let's broach an important yet difficult subject. Why does evil exist? God's ways are mysterious. We might think we have him figured out! As well, we might wonder why we have to live in a world that has so much evil. If we crack open the Catechism, we learn:

> Christian faith as a whole constitutes the answer to this question: the goodness of creation, the drama of sin and the patient love of God who comes to meet man by his covenants, the redemptive Incarnation of his Son, his gift of the Spirit, his gathering of the Church, the power of the sacraments and his call to a blessed life to which free creatures are invited to consent in advance, but from which, by a terrible mystery, they can also turn away in advance. *There is not a single aspect of the Christian message that is not in part an answer to the question of evil.* (CCC, no. 309)

We live in a fallen world, but we should never give in to despair. We should continually pray for strength and understanding. Parents and grandparents can shield the young ones from evil. However, they should also train them to be strong in prayer and foster a loving Christian atmosphere in the home. It is a blessed oasis from the coldness of the world.

> But why did God not create a world so perfect that no evil could exist in it? With infinite power God could always create something better. But with infinite wisdom and goodness God freely willed to create a world "in a state of journeying" toward its ultimate perfection. In God's plan this process of becoming involves the appearance of certain beings and the disappearance of others, the existence of the more perfect alongside the less perfect, both constructive and destructive forces of nature. With physical good there exists also *physical evil* as long as creation has not reached perfection. (CCC, no. 310)

God has gifted each person with a free will. We choose whether we want to be good or evil. Ultimately, we choose whether we desire heaven or hell. It all depends upon our choices and our obedience to God's laws. Talk to the family about their choices. As always, continue to provide a sturdy foundation of Catholic teaching in your domestic church so that the children will have a much better chance of survival out in the world. Even though this is a serious subject, be sure to enjoy some fun today! Find a healthy balance.

PONDER

Remember your Guardian Angel and ask his help. Can you be more mindful of finding opportunities to offer your heart to God and thanking him for countless blessings? God's love shining through you can work miracles in the hearts of others, as well as your own.

FAMILY EVENING PRAYER
to be prayed each evening this week

Dear Lord, thank you for the blessings of this day—your day. If we have failed you in any way, please forgive us. If we have failed one another by not taking care of our responsibilities, please forgive us, Lord. Please help our family to grow in holiness each day. We love you! Amen.

Pray: *Our Father, Hail Mary, Glory Be.*

CHAPTER 47

Relative Sunday

"For this reason I bow my knees before the Father, from whom every family in heaven and on earth takes its name. I pray that, according to the riches of his glory, he may grant that you may be strengthened in your inner being with power through his Spirit, and that Christ may dwell in your hearts through faith, as you are being rooted and grounded in love."
—Ephesians 3:14–17

FAMILY MORNING PRAYER

Read the verse above and pray the Morning Offering together as a family.

Morning Offering: Dear Lord Jesus, thank you for the gift of today— your Sunday. Please guide our family as we strive to grow closer to you and to one another. Open our hearts and teach us to be much more generous with our time. Open our eyes to discover opportunities to love others. Amen.

Pray: *Our Father, Hail Mary, Glory Be.*

REFLECT

Today needs to be all about the family. Could you reach out to your relatives today? I know that we can be well meaning, but then run short of time to make that phone call or make the extra effort for that visit. Time marches on. It doesn't wait for us. We have to seize the opportunity whenever we can so that we will stay connected to our family and extended family. As well, make time to talk with the children about their extended family and their ancestors. If you don't know much about them, this might be the time to do a bit of research.

CHOOSE AN ACTIVITY

Either plan a visit to a relative within driving distance or make a phone call. You might also enjoy video conferencing if you are able. While you're at it, share a recipe, as well as catch up on family news. Older relatives, in particular, will be delighted to hear from you.

Family scrapbook: Make copies of family photos, as well as other meaningful items that you might like to include. Ask the family to make suggestions. You can get as creative as you would like using construction paper, markers, crayons, glitter, and such. Craft stores have an amazing variety of supplies available. The project need not be expensive. Decide in advance if you will gift the finished masterpiece to an older relative who would appreciate it. As well, you can keep it on your own bookshelf. Be sure to date pictures when possible. You might enjoy this project so much that you end up deciding to make another that you can give away!

Family meal: Decide in advance whether you'll be able to bring a home-cooked meal, or at least a special dessert to a relative's home. Or, if they can travel to you, invite them for a family luncheon or dinner. The luncheon idea might be better so that relatives won't have to get home too late in the evening. Get everyone involved in the preparations. Play music. Light candles. Make memories!

NOTE TO PARENTS AND GRANDPARENTS

Talk to the children about the importance of family. I'll never forget my first conversation with Mother Teresa. It was all about the family. When she saw me with my children, she told me that my children were lucky to have a family. She was accustomed to seeing so much dire poverty, and sometimes she rescued babies from dustbins. I looked into her eyes and said, "I am just so blessed to have them." A beautiful conversation unfolded and I thank God for that time we spent conversing. We are all so blessed to be part of a family—no matter what that looks like. Families come in all shapes and sizes. Relish in your family! Let the children know how much you appreciate them.

MINI TEACHING

Parents are coworkers with God. The family has been called the vital cell of society. It is where the Catholic Faith is handed down—right within the walls of our domestic churches. Parents have been called by God to be open to life and to be the first and foremost Faith educators of the children. Our family is actually a community of love. At times, though, it might not look that way! However, so that we don't become discouraged, it's important to remember that we are a work in progress.

In *Evangelium Vitae*, St. John Paul II stated that a family is "a community of life and love, founded upon marriage, and from its mission to 'guard, reveal and communicate love.'" He explained the role of the parents of the family. He stated, "Here it is a matter of God's own love, of which parents are co-workers and as it were interpreters when they transmit life and raise it according to his fatherly plan." How do parents do this? A parent's role is actually heroic. Saint John Paul II stated, "This is the love that becomes selflessness, receptiveness and gift. Within the family each member is accepted, respected and honoured precisely because he or she is a person; and if any family member is in greater need, the care which he or she receives is all the more intense and attentive" (no. 92). Sometimes, it may seem that not much that's noteworthy is happening on a daily basis. It appears to be a lot of plain old ordinariness. Yet, it is there within the family that we help one another to work out our salvation. It is through the give-and-take, the practicing of the virtues, offering love, tenderness, and heaping doses of forgiveness that we grow into what we are meant to be as a family and as human beings.

Saint John Paul II said, "The family has a special role to play throughout the life of its members, from birth to death. It is truly 'the sanctuary of life: the place in which life-the gift of God-can be properly welcomed and protected against the many attacks to which it is exposed, and can develop in accordance with what constitutes authentic human growth.'" He added, "Consequently the role of the family in building a culture of life is decisive and irreplaceable." (*Evangelium Vitae*, no. 92)

PONDER

What are some ways in which you can become more alive in your Faith and express it to others? Will you endeavor to write down three examples? Hang it on your refrigerator to be reminded often. Have fun with the family and make room for playing and laughing! All the while, you are creating marvelous memories for your family.

FAMILY EVENING PRAYER

to be prayed each evening this week

Dear Lord, thank you for the blessings of this day—your day. If we have failed you in any way, please forgive us. If we have failed one another by not taking care of our responsibilities, please forgive us, Lord. Please help us to grow in holiness each day. We love you! Amen.

Pray: *Our Father, Hail Mary, Glory Be.*

CHAPTER 48

Discovery Sunday

"Call to me and I will answer you, and will tell you great
and hidden things that you have not known."
—Jeremiah 33:3

FAMILY MORNING PRAYER

Read the verse above and pray the Morning Offering together as a family.

Morning Offering: Dear Lord Jesus, thank you for the gift of today—
your Sunday. Please guide our family as we strive to grow closer to you
and to one another. Open our hearts and teach us to be much more
generous with our time. Open our eyes to discover opportunities to love
others. Amen.

Pray: *Our Father, Hail Mary, Glory Be.*

REFLECT

Discovery is something quite exciting. Some might say that even our
mistakes can be a reason for discovery. Your whole family could look
at the same thing together, but see something completely different. Of
course, knowledge is a great discovery—learning something brand new.
Parents and grandparents teach and children discover! However, we
should pause to ponder the fact that children teach us and help us to discover something about ourselves as well! What can each family member
discover about themselves?

CHOOSE AN ACTIVITY

Discovery game: Sit together around the kitchen or dining room table. Ask each family member (yes, you too!) to write down at least one hidden talent or a secret desire that they might have. For instance, someone might have the desire to learn to play the piano but has never mentioned it before. Therefore, it is a *secret* desire. Another might wish that they can see the aurora borealis someday. That would be me, by the way!

After you all have completed this task, ask each family member, one at a time, to guess what these things might be for each person. You could ask the person to stand up by their seat while each of the others take a crack at guessing what their hidden talent or secret desire might be. If no one can guess, the person standing can pantomime a clue. They are not permitted to say anything out loud. They can give two more pantomimed clues. If no one guesses, they will announce out loud what the talent or secret desire is. You might all be surprised at what you discover about one another.

Discover yourself: Ask the children to sit still at the table for ten minutes, Set a timer. During their quiet time, they should ponder something that they'd like to discover or that they'd like to accomplish. Give an example to help them get started. They can write down or draw their thoughts on paper.

Discover something new: Ask each family member to spend twenty minutes (or more if needed) today or this week to research (with help) a new subject or even something they might be familiar with but would like to learn more about. Use books you have at home, the internet with supervision, or even a phone call to someone to ask questions. You might decide to take a trip to your local library where you might discover something quite extraordinary. Each family member can share their findings. Everyone will learn, and hopefully, the children will further understand the joy in learning and discovering.

NOTE TO PARENTS AND GRANDPARENTS

Talk to the children about following God's commandments and why that is so necessary in order to get to heaven one day. Help them to discover something new about themselves or someone else, or to learn something new since today is all about "Discovery."

MINI TEACHING

Jesus has told us, "If you wish to enter into life, keep the commandments" (Matt. 19:17). It is our duty to teach our children that there are rules that must be followed. The rules, or commandments, are given to us to protect us—to keep us on the straight and narrow path that leads to heaven. We have the Ten Commandments. As well, Jesus taught the two great commandments of love, the first of which is to love God with all of our hearts, minds, and souls; and the second is like it, to love our neighbor as ourselves. Truly following these commandments of love will keep us from sinning. For, if we sincerely desire to love God and our neighbor, we will work hard in the spiritual life.

Ask the children to list five ways that they can love God and love their neighbor. Have them write them down on paper. Then, ask them at least three ways that they can love themselves. Help them with this.

PONDER

How can you become more alive in your Faith? As you pray, allow God to help you to discover something new about yourself and to help you to be an exemplary Christian example to your family and others. Don't forget to smile (many times!). You are creating marvelous memories for your family. Snap some photos too!

FAMILY EVENING PRAYER

to be prayed each evening this week

Dear Lord, thank you for the blessings of this day—your day. If we have failed you in any way, please forgive us. If we have failed one another by not taking care of our responsibilities, please forgive us, Lord. Please help us to grow in holiness each day. We love you! Amen.

Pray: *Our Father, Hail Mary, Glory Be.*

Works of Mercy Sundays

"And the king will answer them, 'Truly I tell you, just as you did it to one of the least of these who are members of my family, you did it to me.'"
—Matthew 25:40

T he Church teaches that Faith without works is dead. Specifically, we read in the Bible, "What good is it, my brothers and sisters, if you say you have faith but do not have works? Can faith save you? If a brother or sister is naked and lacks daily food, and one of you says to them, "Go in peace; keep warm and eat your fill," and yet you do not supply their bodily needs, what is the good of that? So faith by itself, if it has no works, is dead" (James 2:14–17).

So, we see that Christians must serve others. There is no mincing of words here. Jesus himself came to serve and not to be served. He sets the example for us. The Catechism teaches us that on Sundays we are to refrain from anything that takes away from worshiping God, "the joy proper to the Lord's Day." But also, our activities and busyness should not hinder our "performance of the works of mercy" (CCC, no. 2185). Carrying out works of mercy should be a big part of our lives. This section of *Reclaiming Sundays* will discuss ways in which we can serve God and our neighbor.

CHAPTER 49

Reaching Out Sunday

"On Sundays and other holy days of obligation, the faithful are to refrain from engaging in work or activities that hinder the worship owed to God, the joy proper to the Lord's Day, the performance of the works of mercy, and the appropriate relaxation of mind and body."
—Catechism of the Catholic Church, no. 2185

FAMILY MORNING PRAYER

Read the verse above and pray the Morning Offering together as a family.

Morning Offering: Dear Lord Jesus, thank you for the gift of today—your day. Please guide our family as we strive to grow closer to you and to one another. Open our hearts and teach us to be more generous with our time. Open our eyes to opportunities today to love others. Amen.

Pray: *Our Father, Hail Mary, Glory Be.*

REFLECT

Every Sunday should be about offering mercy to others in one form or another. The problem is that we might pack so many things into our weekends, and most especially our Sundays, that they will prevent us from enjoying the experiences of family, rest, worship, and service. To actually reclaim our Sundays means we need to live countercultural lives, since the world outside our doors has a completely opposite idea. Let's do our best to cut back on our outside activities, unless they include special time with our family, with worship, and service to the needy. As well, when we are home, let's do our best to resist the temptations to pick up devices to check updates, or engage in senseless activities. Rather, we should enjoy our family time and have wholesome conversations. Let's reclaim our Sundays!

CHOOSE AN ACTIVITY

Focus on the hungry: When planning your works of mercy, consider the hungry. Is there a local soup kitchen or food pantry where you can donate food or some time? Could your family choose a Sunday, perhaps today, to make an extra portion of your Sunday dinner to gift to a needy neighbor? Take time with your family to pray and discern where your works of mercy could be most helpful.

Focus on the lonely: Mother Teresa often spoke about the hunger of our Western world. She said that the poverty of spirt and the loneliness in many affluent areas is a far worse disease than the hunger she faced daily in Calcutta, India. Is there someone or a family you know who is struggling financially or in some other way? Could you arrange to bring them a home-cooked meal or needed supplies? Ponder this with your family and try to carry it out soon.

NOTE TO PARENTS AND GRANDPARENTS

Talk to the children about serving Jesus in one another—in other words, doing a work of mercy. Discuss ideas about helping others. It will be helpful for you to prepare your heart by reading Matthew 25:31–46, which you can read aloud at the breakfast table or the dinner table this evening.

MINI TEACHING

Our Lord has instructed us through the Gospel of Matthew (see chapter 25:31–46) to serve him in one another. Jesus tells us, "Whatever you do to the least of these who are members of my family you do to me." Further, we are told that we will be judged at the end of our lives for what we have done and what we have failed to do. Sometimes we might think that our works of mercy must be grand or earth-shattering in some way to be meaningful. But, many of the saints and holy people, including Mother Teresa, have instructed us, "Not all of us can do great things. But we can do small things with great love." And these things are very pleasing to God.

Reflecting on Matthew's Gospel, Mother Teresa also said, "At the end of life we will not be judged by how many diplomas we have received, how much money we have made, how many great things we have done. We will be judged by 'I was hungry, and you gave me something to eat, I was naked and you clothed me. I was homeless, and you took me in.'" (Matthew 25:35).

When you make your lunch or dinner, make an extra portion and put it in a food container that you will gift to someone. It can be an elderly neighbor or a shut-in that you know, a parishioner, or perhaps a relative who would appreciate it. Try your best to deliver the meal soon to whomever you decide should receive it. If not an entire meal, then perhaps you can make a dessert or a fruit plate to give to someone. Encourage the kids to get involved, too, by helping you cook or making a pretty card for the person who will receive the gift.

Addressing the need to feed the hungry doesn't always mean that the recipient has to be starving or homeless. The person might be "hungry" for attention or an act of kindness. Your thoughtful gesture could help them in many ways. Mother Teresa was always quick to point out that countless people in the Western world are starving for love. If you'd like, along with the meal, include a handmade greeting card created by your children.

PONDER

Strive to find ways in which you can become more alive in your faith in doing your works of mercy. As you pray, allow God to transform your heart and soul so you will be an exemplary Christian example to your family and others.

FAMILY EVENING PRAYER
to be prayed each evening this week

Dear Lord, thank you for the blessings of this day—your day. If we have failed you in any way, please forgive us. If we have failed one another by not taking care of our responsibilities, please forgive us, Lord. Please help us to grow in holiness each day. We love you! Amen.

Pray: *Our Father, Hail Mary, Glory Be.*

Showing Mercy Sunday

"I am Love and Mercy itself. When a soul approaches Me with trust, I fill it with such an abundance of graces that it cannot contain them within itself, but radiates them to other souls."
—Jesus to Saint Faustina, *Diary*, no. 1074

FAMILY MORNING PRAYER

Read the verse above and pray the Morning Offering together as a family.

Morning Offering: Dear Lord Jesus, thank you for the gift of today—your Sunday. Please guide our family as we strive to grow closer to you and to one another. Open our hearts and teach us to be much more generous with our time. Open our eyes to discover opportunities to love others. Amen.

Pray: *Our Father, Hail Mary, Glory Be.*

REFLECT

We can get pretty comfortable in our normal routines with not much thought or desire to change anything. Why should we when we feel comfortable, after all? Well, we should because we are Christian. We should because Jesus calls us to move out of our comfort zones to give his love and mercy to others. In today's verse we see that Jesus promises that he will overfill us with his graces when we trust him. He said when he fills a soul with his graces as we trust him, it "cannot contain them . . . but radiates them to other souls." God's love and mercy are boundless. They are everlasting. Will we trust him enough to receive his graces so that we can radiate them to others who are in such need of his mercy? We must ponder that question and then move our wills to step out in faith for our Lord. Let us strive to continually wholeheartedly say, "Jesus, I trust in you."

CHOOSE AN ACTIVITY

Mercy jar. Put your heads and hearts together for this transforming family activity. Gather around the kitchen or dining room table and take turns sharing how you would like to help someone. Is it the people you see holding cardboard signs at intersections? Could it be a neighbor who is lonely after a loss? Is it a student at school who seems unhappy? Have each family member voice out loud and write down (with your help) at least five examples, each on a different slip of paper. Put the finished "mercy petitions" in a large jar to be kept on your kitchen counter. Every morning at breakfast, everyone is encouraged to draw a slip of paper from the "mercy jar." They can then pray about that specific intention and discuss with the family how it might be carried out. At the very least you will be drawing attention to the needs of others and your responsibility to help. Hopefully, this exercise will prod the family to become more merciful people.

NOTE TO PARENTS AND GRANDPARENTS

Talk to the children about the need to think of others' needs and strive to be merciful to them. By spending time together as a family, worshiping God together, learning the Faith, and giving mercy to others today, you will be keeping the Lord's Day holy! As well, try to keep a peaceful environment in your home for a chance for refreshment and rest.

MINI TEACHING

As Christians, we are called to trust in God's mercy. After that, we are to offer mercy to others. To better understand the need to offer mercy, let's take a quick look at God's great mercy and love. It is impossible to completely understand the great mystery of God. However, throughout history, we can see that God has revealed himself and his salvific plan. He spoke to his people through the prophets. The Old and New Testaments reveal God's salvific plan for mankind. He always seeks the salvation of souls.

We know that Jesus came to earth not to be served, but rather (extraordinarily) to serve us! Even though he is God! Because he loves us, he became man and poured out his life upon the Cross to redeem us. When the lance pierced his sacred side, it caused blood and water to gush forth, revealing a fount of mercy for us. Divine Mercy is all about this. We must humble ourselves to receive God's mercy. We must admit our littleness—that we can't survive on our own, that we are sinners. The world tells us something quite opposite. However, we must admit our great need for God's mercy, acknowledging the fact that we are miserable creatures. I know "miserable" might sound too strong or harsh. Yet, truth be told, we are all broken in some way, and all in need of God's mercy.

Divine Mercy is for the whole world—for each and every soul. Jesus told Saint Faustina: "The greater the sinner, the greater the right he has to My mercy" (*Diary*, 723). Jesus gave her three ways to show mercy. He said, "I am giving you three ways of exercising mercy toward your neighbor: the first—by deed, the second—by word, the third—by prayer. In these three degrees is contained the fullness of mercy, and it is an unquestionable proof of love for Me. By this means a soul glorifies and pays reverence to My mercy" (*Diary*, 742). This teaching was not solely for Saint Faustina. It is for all of us.

PONDER

Think of ways that you can be more merciful to others. Could you pause, ponder, and pray before reacting to a rude comment? Could you strive to put others first? How will you show God's mercy to all you encounter this week?

FAMILY EVENING PRAYER
to be prayed each evening this week

Dear Lord, thank you for the blessings of this day—your day. If we have failed you in any way, please forgive us. If we have failed one another by not taking care of our responsibilities, please forgive us, Lord. Please help us to grow in holiness each day. We love you! Jesus, I trust in You! Amen.

Pray: *Our Father, Hail Mary, Glory Be.*

CHAPTER 51

Jesus in Disguise Sunday

"Do everything for the glory of God and the good of His people."
—Mother Teresa, from a letter she wrote to me

FAMILY MORNING PRAYER

Read the verse above and pray the Morning Offering together as a family.

Morning Offering: Dear Lord Jesus, thank you for the gift of today—your Sunday. Please guide our family as we strive to grow closer to you and to one another. Open our hearts and teach us to be much more generous with our time. Open our eyes to discover opportunities to love others. Amen.

Pray: *Our Father, Hail Mary, Glory Be.*

REFLECT

Today's Sunday reflection is titled, "Jesus in Disguise Sunday." What does "distressing disguise" mean? Mother Teresa used the expression "Jesus in the distressing disguise of the poorest of the poor" very often. She wholeheartedly believed that when we serve another, we are really serving Jesus in that person. She fully lived the message in Matthew 25:40, when Jesus said, "Truly I tell you, just as you did it to one of the least of these who are members of my family, you did it to me."

So how does this affect each of us? It is very simple. Jesus asked each person to treat one another with great love and dignity. He told us explicitly in the Gospel of Matthew (please read Matthew) that we are to see him in one another and that we will be judged at the end of our lives according to how well we have loved. It's essential to ponder our lives, our motives, and even our attitudes and to pray to discern how we can improve to please God and help our neighbor.

CHOOSE AN ACTIVITY

"Jesus in Disguise" pantomime or skit: Help the children with very simple performances that they will act out at home. Afterward, discuss how the actions of the actors (if they were people in real life) would impact others' lives. Talk about the need to pray for the people you encounter, as well.

Here are some ideas for skits:

1) Grocery store love: Actor one: You are a young cashier at a grocery store and you are trying to be happy, but you are feeling very depressed because of the loss of someone in your life. Actor two: You are a customer and you don't know of the cashier's life, but you suspect a bit of sadness. What do you do? Do you warmly smile at them? Do you compliment them in an attempt to cheer them up? Will you pray for them afterward? Act this out.

2) Playground bullying: Actor one: You are a bully who continues to pick on "Jesus in disguise" of a smaller child. Actor two: You are the smaller child. Actor Three: You are someone who comes along and intervenes. Act this out.

3) Make your own: Have the children imagine their own "Jesus in disguise" skit!

NOTE TO PARENTS AND GRANDPARENTS

Talk about the need to treat everyone with Christ's love. Read the Gospel of Matthew, chapter 25, to them and discuss what "Jesus in disguise" means. I have no doubt that you will have a very beautiful discussion. Ask the children to name people that they think are "Jesus in disguise." After they have listed some, let them know that *everyone* is "Jesus in disguise." Everyone is created in God's own image and is loved by God. As Catholics, we are to obey God's laws and to love one another.

MINI TEACHING

How do we serve Jesus in others, especially the "least"? These are some ideas I offered, from the life and ministry of Mother Teresa, in my book *Small Things with Great Love*:

Mother Teresa's loving prayerful actions teach us to follow her example. She explained that prayer is imperative to do the work. She taught simply. Holding up her hand, she counted down on her five fingers: "You-did-it-to-Me!" referring to the words in the Gospel of Matthew, "Truly I tell you, just as you did it to one of the least of these who are members of the family, you did it to me" (Matt. 25:40). Her life was a living testament to our Lord's directives to take care of the needy, the naked, the lonely, the poor, the small and insignificant, the most in need. This saint of the gutters changed the world with Christ's love because of her wholehearted "Yes!" to his will, whatever it would be and no matter how hard it was to do. God was always with her even when he seemed distant.

She talked about how Jesus put his love into action. "His love in action for us was the crucifixion," she reflected. She said that she and the Sisters needed to receive Jesus in the Eucharist at Mass each morning in order to have the strength to then take care of the broken bodies of the poor throughout the day. "That gives us the strength and the courage and the joy and the love to touch Him, to love Him, to serve Him. Without Him, we couldn't do it. With Him, we can do all things."

How do each of us serve Jesus in "the least"? For parents, each time you wash your child's face, tie a shoe, feed your babies in the night, bring peace to siblings, provide nutritious meals, or rescue your children from an ungodly culture, you are accomplishing much more than meets the eye when you strive to do it with

244 • *Reclaiming Sundays*

Christ's love. You are certainly serving Jesus in the other. This goes for anyone in any state of life, whether religious or lay. We need to reach out with Christ's love and serve Jesus in those in need in our homes, neighborhoods, workplaces, and communities, and in the strangers we meet.[28]

PONDER

Consider today's teaching, and strive to be more attentive to any needs that unfold around you and to be more cognizant of the fact that Jesus calls us to serve him in others. Ponder ways in which you can grow in your Faith. As you pray, allow God to heal your heart of any hurts.

FAMILY EVENING PRAYER

to be prayed each evening this week

Dear Lord, thank you for the blessings of this day—your day. If we have failed you in any way, please forgive us. If we have failed one another by not taking care of our responsibilities, please forgive us, Lord. Please help us to grow in holiness each day. We love you! Dear Mother Teresa, please pray for us. Amen.

Pray: *Our Father, Hail Mary, Glory Be.*

CHAPTER 52

Anonymous Mercy Sunday

"Blessed are the merciful, for they will receive mercy."
—Matthew 5:7

FAMILY MORNING PRAYER

Read the verse above and pray the Morning Offering together as a family.

Morning Offering: Dear Lord Jesus, thank you for the gift of today—your Sunday. Please guide our family as we strive to grow closer to you and to one another. Open our hearts and teach us to be much more generous with our time. Open our eyes to discover opportunities to love others. Amen.

Pray: *Our Father, Hail Mary, Glory Be.*

REFLECT

Today is about showing mercy, but in an anonymous way. Talk to the family about God's great mercy and the need to continuously show mercy to others. Ask them who they think would benefit from an anonymous act of mercy. Make a list of people and strive to do anonymous merciful acts on a regular basis. Little loving acts can be transformative to both the recipient and the giver! Put your heads together to come up with ideas that would work well. Don't forget about putting this practice into place in your own domestic church!

CHOOSE AN ACTIVITY

Anonymous work of mercy: This can be something tangible or not. For instance, the children might do an act of mercy in being charitable to someone—smiling—listening—loving. Or, they could secretly clean up a sibling's desk, or room, or something that requires another kind of effort.

Mother Teresa often spoke about doing "small things with great love." Little acts of mercy done with love are just as powerful and amazing as larger acts. For instance, the children can straighten out all the hymnals after Sunday Mass. They can hold the door open for someone coming into church or in any public place you might visit. Little things done with love can truly make a difference. Ask the children to think about what they can do. Remind them to put prayer power behind their anonymous actions and not expect thanks. Do it for love!

NOTE TO PARENTS AND GRANDPARENTS

In addition to talking with the family about doing anonymous acts of mercy, talk to the children about the need to be more humble by not trying to take credit when doing good things. Sometimes, it's best that it is between a person and God. No one else has to know. Certainly, we shouldn't parade around about our good deeds. Explain this concept to the children. As well, try to make the day special. It is the Lord's Day, after all. Seize the day! Be blessed and have fun!

MINI TEACHING

Through the Beatitudes, Jesus taught us a special way of life. "Beatitude" means a deep state of joy or happiness. The Beatitudes are the teachings or eight blessings of Jesus in the Sermon on the Mount, which we read about in Matthew 5:1–10. These proclamations of Jesus teach us that if we live according to the Beatitudes as loyal followers, we will live a happy Christian life. Through the eight teachings, Jesus also explains our rewards in our living them out, despite the challenges. The Beatitudes fulfill God's promises made to Abraham and his descendants.

When Jesus saw the crowds, he went up the mountain; and after
he sat down, his disciples came to him. Then he began to
speak, and taught them, saying:
Blessed are the poor in spirit, for theirs is the kingdom of
heaven.
Blessed are those who mourn, for they will be comforted.
Blessed are the meek, for they will inherit the earth.
Blessed are those who hunger and thirst for righteousness, for
they will be filled.
Blessed are the merciful, for they will receive mercy.
Blessed are the pure in heart, for they will see God.
Blessed are the peacemakers, for they will be called children of
God.
Blessed are those who are persecuted for righteousness' sake,
for theirs is the kingdom of heaven.
—Matthew 5:1–10

Take time to read to the family this Scripture passage above. Ask the
family to comment on each Beatitude. You might ask specific questions
and help them with their answers.

What does it mean to hunger and thirst for righteousness?

Who is poor in spirit?

Who are the pure in heart?

Who are the meek? Are you one of them?

Do you know a "peacemaker"? Can you be one?

Do you know anyone who suffered persecution for righteousness'
sake?

Why do the Beatitudes seem contradictory, especially according to
the world's standards? Help them with this to drive home the pure
and essential teachings of Jesus.

PONDER

What are some ways you can become more alive in your Faith and live the Beatitudes? Can you choose one to try and live more fully? As well, have fun with the family today. Make time to relax. Enjoy one another's company. God has certainly blessed the family. Celebrate your family with great love today and always!

FAMILY EVENING PRAYER
to be prayed each evening this week

Dear Lord, thank you for the blessings of this day—your day. If we have failed you in any way, please forgive us. If we have failed one another by not taking care of our responsibilities, please forgive us, Lord. Please help us to grow in holiness each day. We love you! Amen.

Pray: *Our Father, Hail Mary, Glory Be.*

Building Your Domestic Church

"The family, is so to speak, the domestic church."
—*Lumen Gentium*, 11

Catholic families can keep in mind that according to the Second Vatican Council's Dogmatic Constitution on the Church: "The family, is so to speak, the domestic church" (*Lumen Gentium*, no. 11). Catholic parents and grandparents should endeavor to "build" a strong domestic church— equipped to withstand the evil influences from the outside world while being a place of nourishment for the family's souls. We begin building our domestic church through a life of family prayer and love. Consider ways to bring more of the *big* Church into your *little* church. What inspiring images and/or music might you add to your home?

Perhaps, you can add a sacred image, an icon, or a crucifix. These images draw our hearts and minds to the sacred rather than the secular. These holy pictures and objects will help to build a holy foundation in your children's and grandchildren's hearts. The children can make sacred pictures that can be framed and hung in your home. It is a good idea to have a crucifix in each bedroom, perhaps over each bed. The Sacred Heart of Jesus and the Immaculate Heart of Mary are wonderful sacred images to display in family areas of your home.

Be mindful: Building your domestic church is truly a lifelong effort. Try to be mindful of how you are or are not building it up to be a beautiful abode of holiness for your family. Are you setting the tone for holiness? Are you allowing too many influences from the world to enter your home? Can you endeavor to play uplifting worship music at various times?

What prayer times might you incorporate into your days? I like to encourage families to form what I call "prayer habits." Habits might take a while to stick. Therefore, we need to reinforce them. But once you have established certain prayer habits such as Morning and Evening Prayer, the Rosary, a time for Eucharistic Adoration, grace before and after meals, family prayer, and so on, these habits will likely stick with you for life. Laying down this essential foundation for individual prayer and family prayer might be one of the most important spiritual things you do for your family.

Be welcoming: Think about ways to make your domestic church more welcoming to others. Are you sometimes embarrassed when you answer the front door because of nearby clutter that has "mysteriously" accumulated? There have certainly been times when I felt that way. All kinds of things can get dumped by the front door—from sports equipment, book bags, to outerwear. When things are in disarray we might be hesitant to invite someone into our home.

Perhaps you can place a couple of organizational items in your entryway. This might include decorative bins, a shoe tray, or a coat rack. Reinforce the use of these items to keep your entryway neat and de-cluttered. When my kids were young, a decorative basket just inside the front door served to gather knee pads, wrist guards, hats and mittens, and other paraphernalia to keep them from being dropped on the floor or placed elsewhere.

You might consider adding to your foyer or entryway some form of sacred art. In addition to the Irish holy water font beside my front door, a Divine Mercy image hangs in my foyer. As well, a large angel statue sits on the table in my foyer surrounded by old family photos in antique-styled frames. Holy images are inspiring to observe and could catch the eye of a delivery person or a neighbor too. And they have! Beautiful conversations unfold. Naturally, not everyone has the same tastes in design. As you decorate your welcoming space, make it your own and let it exude God's love. Recruit family members to help you tidy up a bit. Perhaps you'll start tomorrow. Put it on your "to-do" list. But make it happen! Once an area is clean and organized, it's easier to keep it that way. Your new entryway can be both tidy and inspiring!

What about certain Catholic traditions?

The blessing of the home: Whether your domestic church is a house or an apartment, invite a priest to come to bless your home. This can be when you first move in or at any time. In addition to the home blessing, you may enthrone your home to the Sacred Heart of Jesus and the Immaculate Heart of Mary. Invite a priest to assist you with the enthronement, or you can do it on your own by hanging up the images in a central location of your home and praying family consecration prayers together. Consider renewing your consecration prayers on a regular basis, perhaps monthly.

You might consecrate your family to the Holy Family of Nazareth. Here is a fitting prayer:

O Lord Jesus, you lived in the home of Mary and Joseph in Nazareth. There you grew in age, wisdom, and grace as you prepared to fulfill your mission as our Redeemer. We entrust our family to you.

O Blessed Mary, you are the Mother of our Savior. At Nazareth you cared for Jesus and nurtured him in the peace and joy of your home. We entrust our family to you.

O Saint Joseph, you provided a secure and loving home for Jesus and Mary, and you gave us a model of fatherhood while showing us the dignity of work. We entrust our family to you.

Holy Family, we consecrate ourselves and our family to you. May we be completely united in a love that is lasting, faithful, and open to the gift of new life. Help us to grow in virtue, to forgive one another from our hearts, and to live in peace all our days. Keep us strong in faith, persevering in prayer, diligent in our work, and generous toward those in need. May our home, O Holy Family, truly become a domestic church where we reflect your example in our daily life. Amen. Jesus, Mary and Joseph, pray for us!

—Composed by Archbishop William E. Lori of Baltimore, Supreme Chaplain of the Knights of Columbus (see http://www.kofc.org/ en/programs/family/consecration-to-the-holy-family.html#/)

Catholic devotions: Praying the Rosary is a popular prayer devotion for many Catholic families, who, through its mysteries, reflect on significant events in Scripture pertaining to Jesus and Mary. While the thought of praying the whole Rosary with small children might seem daunting, it can be done, even just one decade a day to work toward a five-decade Rosary.

Wearing the brown scapular is another popular Catholic devotion whereby the person places himself or herself under the protection of the Blessed Mother. Many popes had a great devotion to the Brown Scapular. Saint John Paul II described the Brown Scapular as being properly clothed by our Mother in heaven. "Our Lady of Mount Carmel dresses us in a spiritual sense. She dresses us with the grace of God and helps us always." It is said that St. John Paul II asked that the doctors not remove his Brown Scapular during his surgery after the assassination attempt in May 1981.

As well, wearing a blessed Miraculous Medal is placing oneself under Mary's protection. The Miraculous Medal is a summary of Church teachings and has its origins through the apparitions of the Blessed Virgin Mary in 1830 to St. Catherine Labouré, a novice with the Daughters of Charity in the Chapel of the Rue du Bac in Paris, France. The Blessed Mother showed the design of the medal to the young nun who was entrusted with the mission of propagating the holy medal. The Blessed Mother explained that she grants great graces to those who wear the medal around their necks. Soon after the first medals were struck and distributed, miracles of physical and emotional health occurred far and wide.

I am very devoted to Our Lady of the Miraculous Medal after receiving several blessed Miraculous Medals from Mother Teresa. I have taken up her practice and have given thousands of Miraculous Medals out to people that I meet. I presently wear one that the humble Saint of the Gutter gave to me as I was enduring a precarious bed-rest pregnancy. She encouraged me to wear it and to call upon Mother Mary often. The doctor did not think that my baby would make it. However, thanks be to God, my baby indeed survived, is now twenty-eight years old, and is named after the Blessed Mother!

Sacred images and sacramentals: As mentioned above, a domestic church should be filled with sacred images and sacramentals. This practice is not merely helping to "build" our domestic church, but sacred images and sacramentals are powerful Catholic devotions. Holy pictures and crucifixes should be hung throughout. You can place a holy water font by the front door in order to bless yourself with holy water and remind you of your Baptism. We bless ourselves with holy water every time we leave our home. Holy water should be regularly sprinkled throughout the home. Saint Teresa said holy water is powerful in expelling demons. Get in the holy habit of blessing your family members with holy water often.

Parental blessings: Parents can trace the Sign of the Cross with their thumb or forefinger (possibly with holy water) on their child's forehead at any time while asking God to bless him or her. Parents and grandparents can put this into practice every evening before bed or whenever they want to invoke God's blessing on the child. The Church teaches, "Every baptized person is called to be a 'blessing,' and to bless. Hence lay people may preside at certain blessings; the more a blessing concerns ecclesial and sacramental life, the more is its administration reserved to the ordained ministry (bishops, priests, or deacons)" (CCC, no. 1669). Perhaps you can begin your parental blessing with a prayer: "The LORD bless you and keep you; the LORD make his face to shine upon you, and be gracious to you; the LORD lift up his countenance upon you, and give you peace" (Num. 6:24–26).

Celebrate name days: Celebrate your family's name days, which are the days dedicated to each person's patron saint. Our name is important to God. The Church teaches, "God calls each one by name. Everyone's name is sacred. The name is the icon of the person. It demands respect as a sign of the dignity of the one who bears it" (CCC, no. 2158). Celebrating name days has been a custom in Catholic countries in Europe and South America for centuries. Immigrants have carried it into North America. By forming your own family tradition in observing your children's name days, you will focus on their patron saints, seek the saints' intercession and protection, instill a wonderful practice in your family, and have a holy reason to celebrate!

Follow the liturgical year: Families can pray the Liturgy of the Hours together. The liturgical calendar is structured around the life of Christ and the lives of his followers. Folks who follow the calendar by praying the Liturgy of the Hours have expressed that they felt more connected to the Church. Praying in this way brings divine meaning into each day.

As always, let me encourage you also to establish your own family traditions. Most especially, enjoy regular dinners together, connecting as a family, sharing and praying together. You will be setting down a wonderful foundation for your family, showing them the importance of time together. Hopefully, they'll carry this tradition into their own homes later on.

ACKNOWLEDGMENTS

I am deeply grateful to my parents, Eugene Joseph and Alexandra Mary Cooper, for bringing me into the world and raising me in a large Catholic family, and to my grandmother Alexandra Mary Uzwiak for setting a beautiful prayerful example. And thank you to my brothers and sisters— Alice Jean, Gene, Gary, Barbara, Tim, Michael, and David—for being a wonderful part of my life.

My heartfelt gratitude goes to my husband, Dave, and my beloved children—Justin, Chaldea, Jessica, Joseph, and Mary-Catherine— for their continued love and support, and to my precious grandsons, Shepherd and Leo. I love you all dearly.

I am deeply grateful to my friend, Servant of God Father John Hardon, sj, who spiritually directed and encouraged me, and is no doubt continuing from heaven. Also, an exuberant thank you to dear Mother Teresa for playing a huge role in shaping me spiritually, which I know she continues even now, and to Father Andrew Apostoli, CFR, a dear friend and spiritual director, now helping me from heaven.

I owe very special thanks to Paraclete Press, to Jon Sweeney, and to Robert Edmonson, and all the wonderful team at Paraclete Press that helped get this book out to you!

Finally, I am extremely thankful for my readership, viewership, and listenership, and to all those I meet in my travels. I pray for you every day. Thank you for being part of my fascinating journey through life. Please pray for me too. May God bless you in great abundance!

APPENDIX 1

Meaningful Family Activities

"So let us not grow weary in doing what is right, for we will reap at harvest time, if we do not give up."
—Galatians 6:9

Throughout this book you have seen many suggestions for Sunday family activities. I have added additional choices in this section. Hopefully, some will pique your interest. Perhaps they might also inspire you to come up with ideas of your own. Some activities will be related to works of mercy, and others will be educational or just plain wholesome fun. Whatever you do together, enjoy it and try not to be concerned about perfection. Ultimately, you will be experiencing and discovering new things together, as well as creating warm memories too!

WORKS OF MERCY ACTIVITIES

1) Baby Shower

I have carried this out in my own parish, and it worked very well. Could you consider a family project or activity that supports life? How about arranging a "baby shower" that can be held at your parish in the near future to benefit a local pro-life pregnancy center? You can seek permission from your pastor, then put a notice in the parish bulletin asking for donations of new baby items (possibly specifying a few important ones), noting the dates and times for folks to drop off their donated items. You and your family, as well as any others you might enlist to help, can collect the gifts and deliver them. The center will surely be most delighted as well as grateful to receive the practical gifts.

2) Surprise Meal

Gift a homemade meal to a family with a new baby, a family enduring struggle or sickness, or anyone who could use perking up and nourishment. Get the whole family involved in planning and cooking. Encourage them to make a colorful drawing or warm greeting card to go along with the meal. Deliver the meal with smiling faces to warm the hearts of the recipients.

3) Clothing Drive

Research the needs in your area (or another area) and carry out a clothing drive to benefit the needy. Announce it in the parish bulletin a month ahead of the event. Be specific about the types of clothing you are collecting and where it will be delivered. Give a couple of sentences to explain the need. Ask for donations for shipping costs as well, if the items cannot be delivered personally. Set a date (if not the date of the event) for volunteers to help pack the items into boxes to be delivered or shipped to the recipients. One possibility of a need might be the folks who eat at the local soup kitchen. In the past, I've arranged for a collection of warm clothing that was delivered to the soup kitchen at the time the guests arrived to eat. They were free to choose whatever they would like. If you live in a cold area, you might like to specify that you'd like to collect gloves, hats, scarves, and warm socks for men, women, and children.

4) Toiletry Collection Drive

If there is a soup kitchen in your area, you can look into donating these sorts of items, also, for the guests there. They might not usually receive items that they could use for hygiene: small bottles of shampoo, toothpaste, toothbrushes, combs, brushes, soap, and the like. The less fortunate would also appreciate gift cards to a coffee house or fast-food restaurant. Plan a collection of these types of items at your parish after seeking permission from the pastor. Post it in the bulletin at least a month in advance with a couple of more reminders. You might even have the children make a nice, bright, colorful poster with pertinent details that you can help them add to the poster. Hang it in your parish hall. After the items have been donated, arrange a time with the local soup kitchen or social-service department to deliver the items.

OTHER ACTIVITIES

Make a Saint Recipe!

This activity requires a bit of research to decide what kinds of foods the saints enjoyed. Perhaps you'll make a recipe that was common in the area and time that your saint lived. Or, perhaps you'll make something like an Irish soda bread to remember Saint Patrick. Have fun researching and deciding what you'd like to make together. Put it on your calendar. Maybe every First Saturday will become "Saints' Recipe Day." You decide!

Letter Writing

Yes, old-fashioned letter writing. You might ask, "Is this still a thing?" Who actually writes a letter nowadays, when we have email and the internet? Well, I say we should bring it back! I certainly love and appreciate receiving a handwritten letter. It shows me the love that went into it. Perhaps this is something you can do monthly. Get the family together at the kitchen or dining room table. Ask each family member to list three people that could use encouragement. Compile all the suggestions onto a main list. Find stationery paper at home or purchase some soon. Start writing! It's that simple. You can share ideas about what a comforting letter would entail and put pen (or crayon or marker) to paper and write with your heart!

Scavenger Hunt or Treasure Hunt

There is a difference between a treasure hunt in which you hide things to be found, and a scavenger hunt when you don't. The treasure hunt could be comprised of little treasures such as candy or trinkets, books, or any treat that the finder gets to keep! You will hide these items in advance of the game. You could make a treasure map or simply a list of the items they must find. The scavenger hunt is carried out by finding things that are on a list that you will make of about ten or twelve items. These are items that are already there. You don't need to hide items. You will make and distribute the list to the people doing the scavenger hunt. The first person who finds all the items is the winner. In advance, you can just walk through an area of your home, yard, or park, or wherever you will play the game, and simply jot the items on your list. Perhaps the winner will be rewarded with a prize! The list can consist of things such as a clothespin, a hairbrush, something shiny, a dollar bill, a pet, a marble. If you are outside, the items might be things such as an orange leaf, a shiny twig, a smooth pebble, bark from a tree, a daffodil. Have fun!

Board Games

Board games are always a good idea for family fun. Sadly, we might feel we have no time to comfortably sit down and enjoy a good board game. That's why it's important to carve out the time. Make your own board game or use what you have on hand. We have a whole closet filled with board games. We try to play at least one every time the "kids" come home. I hope to play them with my grandchildren as well. I challenge you not only to make the time for fun and educational board games that you might already have at home, but also to create one! That will definitely be a great adventure. You can put your heads together to decide what kind of game it will be and then set out to create it. You can use cardboard and construction paper, markers, and craft supplies. Have fun!

Time Capsule

We mentioned this one briefly, earlier in this book. Plan to make a time capsule with your family. A few things to ponder: Would you put a dated note inside along with pertinent items? Where would you put it? Would you bury it? Even if you won't carry this out, it will be fun to plan it. Or, you might make it and store it in an attic or bookshelf to be opened at a certain date. In that case, mark the outside of the container with the date so you won't forget. Ask each family member what they could add to the capsule that would represent their personality. You can have a lot of fun with this activity!

Family Cookbook or Recipe Box

Since family time should be a lot about gathering together around the table to break bread and share hearts, documenting favorite recipes should be enjoyable. This is one of those activities that you'll be thanking yourself later on for putting in the effort now. I encourage you to reach out to older relatives, if possible, to ask for their favorite recipes, and then try to make them soon. A few ideas for making your cookbook or recipe box:

Write or type the recipes, and add a few comments from the family about how they enjoyed the dish.

Be sure to include a relative's name if they have shared the recipe.

Set aside at least a few Sundays to work on this project. It can certainly be an ongoing effort, as you will likely try new recipes over time.

Write a Family Story

We did this one time when my children were young. One summer day while cooling off in a pool, we decided to write a story. Each of us took turns and told a part of the story. We wrote it down as we went around and around to each person, who then added to what was previously said. You will be amazed at what you can all put together. This fun activity gets everyone thinking and contributing. The end result might be quite hilarious or even serious and inspiring. Make up your own ways to write stories, as well. Perhaps each family member will have their own chapter. Enjoy crafting it and reading it out loud when it's completed.

Trips and Pilgrimages

Family trips are fun and can be stressful too. It's not always easy to travel because everyone is out of their usual routine and away from the comfort of home. Be prepared for it to be difficult for certain family members to adjust to change. Make allowances for cranky moods, all the while correcting, encouraging—and praying! A fun and meaningful trip can be as simple as going to the local library to read stories or just browse.

A change of scenery is always refreshing. You might even stop for ice cream or frozen yogurt on the way there! Take time soon to plan at least a few simple, yet educational and fun family trips. Write them down and post the ideas on the refrigerator. Or, write your destination goals on a bulletin or dry-erase board. Seeing them will remind you to carve out the time to embark upon those adventures!

Think about pilgrimages, as well. A short trip to a local shrine or basilica can turn into a memorable and enriching pilgrimage. As well, you might decide to travel farther on a pilgrimage. A pilgrimage is a lot about *getting to* the destination, which is just about as important as being there. Strive to create a prayerful and fun atmosphere while traveling there. A few ideas:

1. Be sure to include prayer along the journey.

2. Research in advance to enhance the understanding of the holy place to be visited.

3. Give each family member a particular responsibility along the trip.

Family Luncheon or Dinner

Have the children plan a family luncheon or dinner from soup to nuts! Write down the recipes that you come up with, and add them to your family recipe box or cookbook. If it works out well, think about doing it again and invite a relative! A few ideas:

1. Keep expectations low.

2. Don't worry about a mess!

3. Get everyone involved in clean up afterward.

4. Light a candle on the dinner table to create a more festive atmosphere.

5. Play classical or soothing music while eating.

Rest and Be Refreshed

Resting is a wonderful thing. It's also very therapeutic, and quite honestly, it's necessary for survival. However, most people tend to neglect this important "activity." Additional ideas for ways to rest:

1. Spread a blanket on the living room or family room floor, sit on it, and play a game, read books, or tell a story. Take deep breaths and enjoy.

2. Everyone can lie on their bed and take a half-hour nap.

3. Play soothing music, while everyone closes their eyes for fifteen minutes.

4. Pray a slow decade of the Rosary together. Close your eyes.

5. Go outside, weather permitting, sit in the sunshine, and breathe in the fresh air.

6. Tell a story about your childhood.

7. Tell jokes.

Crafts

If there is a craft store nearby, just walking around and looking at the amazing selection of arts and crafts supplies could get the wheels turning in your brain! Here are a few ideas to get you started:

1) Planting Flowers, Painting Flower Pots, and Drawing Plants

This family activity is perfect for a rainy-day Sunday. However, you can do it at any time. Gather your art supplies and decide upon a time when you can sit together with the children and decorate flowerpots with markers, paints, or crayons. Fill three decorated flowerpots about three-quarters full with potting soil, and plant the desired flower or vegetable seeds in the pots. Water the seeds, and place the pots in a sunny window or area of your home. Remember to water the seeds about two or three times a week. One flower pot can be used as a gift for someone, another can be used on a prayer table in your home in honor of the Blessed

Mother (especially if you are in the month of May), and the third can be placed somewhere in your home.

If you would rather not plant seeds, have the children draw pictures of plants growing in a garden or a field with a gentle rain coming down on the plants. Talk to the children about nature, God, and how the rain and sun help to make the plants grow. Hang their pictures up high on an "arts and crafts line," which you can make by stringing a thin rope or sturdy string (complete with clothespins) in a safe area of your kitchen or family area to display your family's artwork. As well, you can put the works of art on a bulletin board or on the refrigerator.

2) Family Scrapbook

This fun activity is perfect for any time of year and any weather. You'll be glad that you carved out the time to make it happen. Make copies of favorite family photos, as well as other meaningful items that you might like to include. Ask the family to make suggestions. Also, ask their comments about the photos and write them as quotes under the photo after you put it in the scrapbook. For instance, "Johnny said, 'This was one of the best days ever!'" You can get as creative as you would like using construction paper, markers, crayons, glitter, and such. Craft stores have an amazing variety of supplies available. The project need not be expensive. Decide in advance if you will gift the finished masterpiece to an older relative who would appreciate it. As well, you can keep it on your own bookshelf. Be sure to date pictures when possible. You might want to make two—one to give away and one to keep.

3) Saint Puppets

This activity is appropriate at any time. Perhaps you might do it in late October or in early November when we celebrate the feast of All Saints on November 1. However, since the saints are always relevant, you can do this at any time. Think about what saints you would like to make into puppets! Pull out a saint book or do a little research online to learn more about the saints you choose. Use construction paper or colored felt, markers, fabric paint, glitter, glue, and anything you'd like to create simple or elaborate saint puppets. After the glue or paint has dried, have the children put on a skit with the puppets. Perhaps you will make popcorn and enjoy the show!

4) Saint Movie

This activity won't require much effort except deciding together upon which movie to watch! Pop some popcorn and possibly get some other snacks ready, and carve the time to sit down together to enjoy a wonderful saint movie. Make it happen!

APPENDIX 2

Resources

The Catechism of the Catholic Church: http://www.vatican.va/archive /ENG0015/_INDEX.HTM.

Dogmatic Constitution on the Church (*Lumen Gentium*): http://www. vatican.va/archive/hist_councils/ii_vatican_council/documents/vat-ii _const_19641121_lumen-gentium_en.html.

The Role of the Christian Family in the Modern World (*Familiaris Consortio*): http://w2.vatican.va/content/john-paul-ii/en/apost_exhortations /documents/hf_jp-ii_exh_19811122_familiaris-consortio.html.

Pastoral Constitution on the Church in the Modern World (*Gaudium et Spes*): http://www.vatican.va/archive/hist_councils/ii_vatican_council /documents/vat-ii_cons_19651207_gaudium-et-spes_en.html.

Evangelium Vitae ("The Gospel of Life"): http://w2.vatican.va/content /john-paul-ii/en/encyclicals/documents/hf_jp-ii_enc_25031995_evangelium -vitae.html.

"The Domestic Church: The Catholic Home" at "Fish Eaters": https:// www.fisheaters.com/domesticchurch.html.

NOTES

1   Source: https://www.plough.com/en/topics/culture/poetry/six-poems-for-spring and here: https://www.poets.org/poetsorg/poem/prayer-spring.

2   Pope John Paul II, *The Gospel of Life*, from the encyclical *Evangelium Vitae* (New York: Times Books/Random House, 1995).

3   *Familiaris Consortio*, Part Three, number 18: http://w2.vatican.va/content/john-paul-ii/en/apost_exhortations/documents/hf_jp-ii_exh_19811122_familiaris-consortio.html.

4   Apostolic Letter: DIES DOMINI: May 31, 1998, Pope John Paul II: https://w2.vatican.va/content/john-paul-ii/en/apost_letters/1998/documents/hf_jpii_apl_05071998_dies-domini.html.

5   This quotation is from an article in *Epic Pew*: https://epicpew.com/holy-water/.

6   *Catholic Exchange* article, excerpt from Rev. Henry Theiler, *Holy Water and Its Significance for Catholics* (Bedford, NH: Sophia Institute Press, 2016): https://catholicexchange.com/effects-holy-water.

7   Visitation Sisters, *Thoughts and Sayings of St. Margaret Mary,* (Charlotte, NC: TAN Books, 1990), 14.

8   Source: "Lent 1982," Catholic News Agency: https://www.catholicnewsagency.com/document/lent-1982-9557.

9   Pope John Paul II, Angelus, November 30, 1986: https://w2.vatican.va/content/john-paul-ii/en/apost_letters/1998/documents/hf_jpii_apl_05071998_dies-domini.html.

10 See "Sunday Mass and Holy Day Obligation:" https://www.ewtn.com/expert/answers/sunday_mass.htm.

11 Saint Margaret Mary Alacoque, *The Letters of St. Margaret Mary Alacoque: Apostle of the Sacred Heart* (Charlotte, NC: TAN Books, 1954), 28.

12 Henry Dieterich, *Through the Year with Fulton Sheen* (San Francisco: Ignatius, 2003), 28.

13 Saint Maria Faustina Kowalska, *Divine Mercy in My Soul* (Stockbridge, MA: Marian Press, 2005), 742.

14 http://www.usccb.org/prayer-and-worship/prayers-and-devotions/mary/index.cfm.

15 Donna-Marie Cooper O'Boyle, *Our Lady's Messages to the Three Shepherd Children and the World* (Bedford, NH: Sophia Institute Press, 2017).

16 Source: https://www.ewtn.com/expert/answers/apparitions.htm.

17 Source: https://www.ewtn.com/expert/answers/apparitions.htm.

18 http://www.usccb.org/prayer-and-worship/prayers-and-devotions/mary/index.cfm.

19 Source: https://www.osv.com/OSVNewsweekly/ByIssue/Article/TabId/735/ArtMID/13636/ArticleID/10312/What-Catholics-need-to-know-about-making-their-homes-a-domestic-church.aspx.

20 Paul Thigpin, *A Dictionary of Quotes from the Saints* (Charlotte, NC: TAN Books, 2001), 250.

21 *Crisis Magazine*, March 1, 1998, "Saints who Laugh," https://www.crisismagazine.com/1998/saints-who-laugh, n.p.

22 Source: *Saints*: http://www.usccb.org/prayer-and-worship/prayers-and-devotions/saints/.

23 Source: *Saints*: http://www.usccb.org/prayer-and-worship/prayers-and-devotions/saints/.

24   Donna-Marie Cooper O'Boyle, *52 Weeks with Saint Faustina: A Year of Grace and Mercy* (Stockbridge, MA: Marian Press, 2019), 23.

25   Kowalska, *Divine Mercy in My Soul,* 47–48.

26   Kowalska, *Divine Mercy in My Soul,* 299.

27   Source: "Prayer and Worship: Ordinary Time," USCCB: http://www.usccb.org/prayer-and-worship/liturgical-year/ordinary-time.cfm

28   Donna-Marie Cooper O'Boyle, *Small Things with Great Love: A 9-Day Novena to Mother Teresa the Saint of the Gutters* (Brewster, MA: Paraclete Press, 2019), 30.

ABOUT THE AUTHOR

Donna-Marie Cooper O'Boyle is a Catholic wife, mother of five children, a grandmother, and an award-winning and best-selling author and journalist, TV host, international speaker, and pilgrimage and retreat leader. She is the EWTN television host of *Everyday Blessings for Catholic Moms*, *Catholic Mom's Cafe*, and *Feeding Your Family's Soul*, which she created to teach, encourage, and inspire Catholic families. Her love of children and teaching the Faith has motivated her as a catechist for nearly thirty years. She is also an Extraordinary Minister of the Eucharist at her parish. Donna-Marie was noted as one of the Top Ten Most Fascinating Catholics in 2009 by *Faith & Family Live*. She was invited by the Holy See to participate in an international congress for women at the Vatican to mark the twentith anniversary of the apostolic letter *Mulieris Dignitatem* (On the Dignity and Vocation of Women). She enjoyed a decade-long friendship with Mother Teresa of Calcutta and became a Lay Missionary of Charity. For many years her spiritual director was Servant of God John A. Hardon, SJ, who also served as one of Mother Teresa's spiritual directors.

Donna-Marie is the author of more than thirty books on faith and family, including *Feeding Your Family's Soul*, *The Miraculous Medal*, *Angels for Kids*, and her memoir, *The Kiss of Jesus: How Mother Teresa and the Saints Helped Me to Discover the Beauty of the Cross*. She has been profiled on many television shows, including Fox News, *Rome Reports*, Vatican *Insider*, *Women of Grace*, *Sunday Night Prime*, *EWTN Live*, *At Home with Jim and Joy*, *The Journey Home*, and *Faith & Culture* on EWTN. Donna-Marie lives with her family in beautiful rural New England, and she lectures throughout the world on topics relating to Catholic and Christian women, faith, and families, the saints, and her friend Mother Teresa. She can be reached at her websites: www.donnacooperoboyle.com and www.feedingyourfamilyssoul.com, where you can learn more about Donna-Marie's books, ministry, and pilgrimages, and where she also maintains blogs.

ABOUT PARACLETE PRESS

Who We Are

As the publishing arm of the Community of Jesus, Paraclete Press presents a full expression of Christian belief and practice—from Catholic to Evangelical, from Protestant to Orthodox, reflecting the ecumenical charism of the Community and its dedication to sacred music, the fine arts, and the written word. We publish books, recordings, sheet music, and video/DVDs that nourish the vibrant life of the church and its people.

What We Are Doing

Books

PARACLETE PRESS BOOKS show the richness and depth of what it means to be Christian. While Benedictine spirituality is at the heart of who we are and all that we do, our books reflect the Christian experience across many cultures, time periods, and houses of worship.

We have many series, including *Paraclete Essentials*; *Paraclete Fiction*; *Paraclete Poetry*; *Paraclete Giants*; and for children and adults, *All God's Creatures*, books about animals and faith; and *San Damiano Books*, focusing on Franciscan spirituality. Others include *Voices from the Monastery* (men and women monastics writing about living a spiritual life today), *Active Prayer*, and new for young readers: *The Pope's Cat*. We also specialize in gift books for children on the occasions of Baptism and First Communion, as well as other important times in a child's life, and books that bring creativity and liveliness to any adult spiritual life.

The MOUNT TABOR BOOKS series focuses on the arts and literature as well as liturgical worship and spirituality; it was created in conjunction with the Mount Tabor Ecumenical Centre for Art and Spirituality in Barga, Italy.

Music

The PARACLETE RECORDINGS label represents the internationally acclaimed choir *Gloriæ Dei Cantores*, the *Gloriæ Dei Cantores Schola*, and the other instrumental artists of the *Arts Empowering Life Foundation*.

Paraclete Press is the exclusive North American distributor for the Gregorian chant recordings from St. Peter's Abbey in Solesmes, France. Paraclete also carries all of the Solesmes chant publications for Mass and the Divine Office, as well as their academic research publications.

In addition, PARACLETE PRESS SHEET MUSIC publishes the work of today's finest composers of sacred choral music, annually reviewing over 1,000 works and releasing between 40 and 60 works for both choir and organ.

Video

Our video/DVDs offer spiritual help, healing, and biblical guidance for a broad range of life issues including grief and loss, marriage, forgiveness, facing death, understanding suicide, bullying, addictions, Alzheimer's, and Christian formation.

Learn more about us at our website:
www.paracletepress.com
or phone us toll-free at 1.800.451.5006

YOU MAY ALSO BE INTERESTED IN THESE BY
Donna-Marie Cooper O'Boyle . . .

FEEDING YOUR FAMILY'S SOUL
Dinner Table Spirituality

ISBN 978-1-61261-835-7 | $15.99, Trade paperback

A CATHOLIC WOMAN'S BOOK OF PRAYERS
ISBN 978-1-61261-921-7 | $11.99, Trade paperback

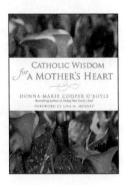

CATHOLIC WISDOM FOR A MOTHER'S HEART
ISBN 978-1-61261-922-4 | $13.99, Trade paperback

Available at bookstores

Paraclete Press | 1-800-451-5006 | www.paracletepress.com